SEXUAL EXERCISES FOR
WOMEN

Dr. A. HARRIS

Carroll & Graf Publishers, Inc.
New York

Published in Great Britain by Quartet Books Ltd

First edition published in the United States by Carroll & Graf Publishers Inc.

Carroll & Graf Publishers, Inc.
260 Fifth Avenue
New York, NY 10001

Library of Congress Cataloging-in-Publication Data

Harris, Anthony, 1937–
  Sexual exercises for women.

  1. Exercise for women. 2. Sex. I. Title.
RA781.H36 1988   613.7'1'088054   88-7341
ISBN: 0-88184-412-8

Manufactured in the United States of America

CONTENTS

INTRODUCTION

This book is dedicated to women. Its purpose is to enhance physical and mental wellbeing through an entirely new concept of fitness and health based on a revolutionary exercise technique called Sexual Exercises.

When I first began giving exercise classes, I concentrated on techniques for body shaping. It was only when my women students came to me and told me about the other benefits arising from these routines that I went on to develop the Sexual Exercises, which are designed to cater for the specific needs of the female body and to mobilize its considerable resources.

The physical effects of Sexual Exercises are feeling good with improved muscle tone. This occurs when the body is flushed throughout with endorphins, the pleasure-giving hormones. These are so powerful that they can actually obliterate pain and replace it with pleasure.

Because for most people pleasure in the body is only momentarily experienced, and only then during sexual activity, this pleasure is often called sexual pleasure, but actually sexual pleasure is merely one small part of the general health pleasure. Sexual Exercises mobilize your own body resources for feeling good all the time. The aim of Sexual Exercises is to teach you to know and enjoy your own body, and to develop your awareness of and pleasure in it.

Sexual Exercises are liberating. A knowledge of your body can bring with it a freedom that can have an enormously beneficial effect on your sexual life. A woman who has suffered at the hands of a clumsy or inept lover may dread the thought of making love and may feel that she is responsible for the failure. Through these exercises, she can rediscover her own body and learn about her own capacity for pleasure, which will compensate for past difficulties.

It is also important to find out which areas of your body are most responsive and in what way. These vary greatly from woman to woman and, as you become more familiar with your body and its sensitivities through Sexual Exercises, so you will learn how you most like to be caressed and where your areas of maximum pleasure lie. You can put this knowledge to good use. Teach your lover to know your body as you know it yourself.

Many women assume that any pleasure they experience while making love is the gift of their lover. If the affair breaks up, the woman feels that she has lost the possibility of sexual pleasure. Through Sexual Exercises, she will discover that she is the mistress of her own enjoyment. This autosexuality, which means, literally, sexual feelings through oneself, should not be confused with masturbation, which is often associated with fantasy, and is usually genital rather than holistic, quite different from Sexual Exercises. Sexual Exercises enhance health.

Your body has nerve endings both inside and out which respond to stimuli such as a touch, a caress, heat, cold, moisture, the sensation of silk. Your senses are also responsive to stimuli – what you hear, see, taste, touch and smell. A low-level stimulus given over a long period of time will produce the same effect as a strong stimulus over a short period. For example, stroking the breast gently will eventually result in increased blood flow, but stronger deeper massage will create the same effect more quickly. The level of the sexual response depends on the strength of the stimulus and a mild response can develop into a major one if further stimulus is received. Stimuli can reinforce and complement one another. Your enjoyment of a massage, for instance, can be enhanced by the use of aromatic oils. When you are doing Sexual Exercises, exploit this principle – play music, use perfume, place yourself in a pleasing and sensual environment.

When the stimulus is received, the endorphin levels rise and blood flows to the breasts, the vagina, the uterus and all the sexual parts. This flow of sexual energy is experienced as a very pleasant feeling and is indeed the basis for the sensation of joy one experiences in being alive.

It is important to distinguish between sexual excitement, as described above, and sexual tension which is a blocking of sexual energy in which the muscles become unhealthily rigid and sometimes knotted. In health, the muscles are soft and springy to the touch.

Sexual tension occurs when sexual excitement

reaches an intense pitch and is not discharged. The release or discharge of sexual energy can occur through orgasm. Stress then is an unrelieved stimulus caused by sexual energy being blocked in tight muscles and cramped postures, instead of being expressed in healthy movement or even joyous hard work, as well as in sexual acts. It takes little imagination to understand that chronically blocking sexual energies can lead to ill health. The aim of Sexual Exercises is to let your energies flow. Sexual Exercises are a means to health, and, as such, are not primarily concerned with sexual pleasure or sexual acts with partners, although they do have the result of increasing both pleasure and satisfaction.

A woman's sexuality is a mysterious and private thing, and, for this reason, you will get the best from the exercises if you do them when you are alone. Privacy, like company, is more than a luxury, it is a basic human need. Given the intimate nature of the exercises, you will find yourself best able to respond if you feel truly relaxed and uninhibited.

The only exception to this is if you are pregnant. We have found that pregnant women, while often benefiting from the less strenuous exercises, are best advised to do them in a group. A pregnant woman should consult her doctor before embarking upon the exercises.

Women who habitually suffer from menstrual cramps report that, after doing the exercises over several months, they no longer get pains. They also claim to feel sexier during their periods. As the purpose of the exercises is to encourage a better relationship with your body, it may well be that the stresses and strains, both mental and physical, that are often associated with menstruation, are alleviated by increased awareness and relaxation.

HOW TO USE THE BOOK

Sexual Exercises involve a method based on research in which the classical scientific pattern of observation, experimentation and, finally, creation, was adhered to. The effects of the exercises are the reported experiences of the women who helped me with this research.

I have divided the book into three main parts: Basics, General Exercises, and Specific Exercises.

BASICS introduces you to your body. It covers essential areas of scientific and anatomical knowledge which, because they are explained through illustrations and observations of your own body and its responses, are easy to understand. The majority of women find this section best to begin with.

GENERAL EXERCISES incorporates methods of strengthening and toning your whole body, and introduces the first of the Sexual Exercises. This is essential for every woman.

SPECIFIC EXERCISES teaches you to work on a particular part of your body in order to achieve harmony throughout the whole body. Some women can start here and derive benefit although the general exercises need to be studied first.

I found that this arrangement was most successful in my seminars and classes. A mixture of theory and practice is best. While you are actually exploring and developing your own body, you are also learning the science behind the technique. Hasten slowly, do everything gently, and, above all, don't rush.

PART ONE: BASICS

1. EXPLAINING ENDORPHINS

The existence of hormones which regulate an internal network of pleasurable sensations has now been proved, so we know that delight is chemical although we experience it as emotion. The brain and certain nerve-centres produce endorphins which are very simple protein-like molecules that give sensations ranging from pleasure to ecstasy. When you are healthy, you have a high level of endorphins in your body which literally make you feel good. When you are depressed or unhealthy, the level drops with a corresponding drop in your sense of wellbeing.

You must recognize that pain, discomfort, anxiety and muscular tension are all warning signs that your equilibrium is being upset. Quite literally, any physical or mental state that is not pleasurable or balanced, is one of dis-equilibrium, which is one step away from dis-ease. Learn that pleasure is a sign of health.

If you are exhausted, the level of many endorphins in your body will be low. If you are healthy, it is high. Endorphins have a complex role, in that some are pain-killers, others are pleasure-givers, but the level of all depends on physical and mental stimulus. Sexual Exercises are powerful stimuli.

There are at least twenty endorphins which are produced in the brain and nerve-centres, of which there are many in the pelvic region, from the proteins in our food. Once in the bloodstream, amino acids from protein can be carried to the brain or nerve concentrations and used to make endorphins. They are then carried by the blood stream to all parts of your body.

Certain kinds of movement, such as dancing, swimming, walking and, not least, making love, give pleasure. We can therefore conclude that these movements affect hormone levels. We all know that competitive movement, as in sport, causes the adrenalin levels to rise, and, by the same token, certain kinds of serene balanced bodily activity can stimulate the endorphin levels. Sexual Exercises enhance pleasure and serenity, while combating stress. Stress reduces the levels of the pleasure hormones.

2. GETTING TO KNOW YOUR BODY

Sexual energy flows through the nerves, the blood and lymph vessels, along the muscles and over the skin. These pathways are activated by Sexual Exercises, and your first step towards getting the most from the facts and discoveries in this book is to understand how your body works. So strip off in a warm room with a large mirror and settle down to a home anatomy lesson.

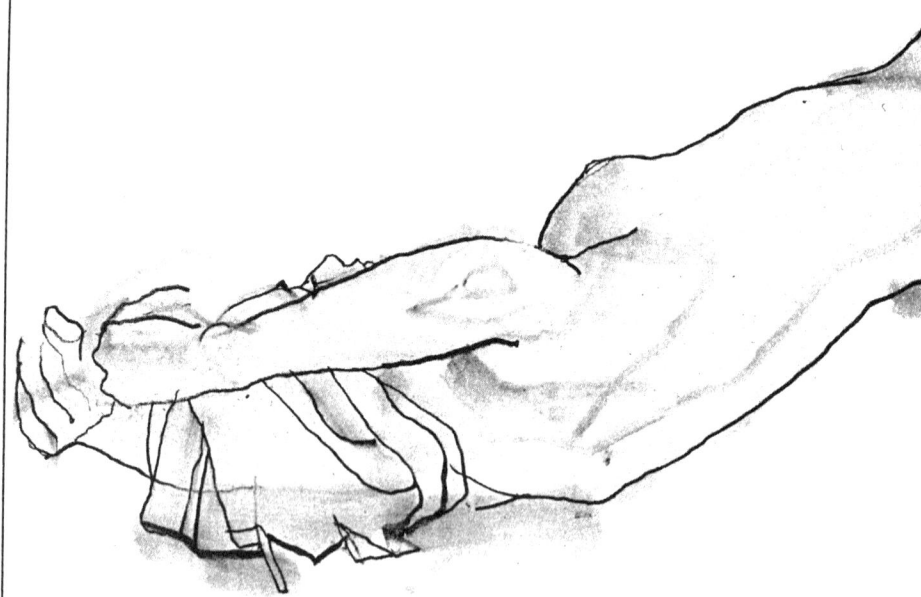

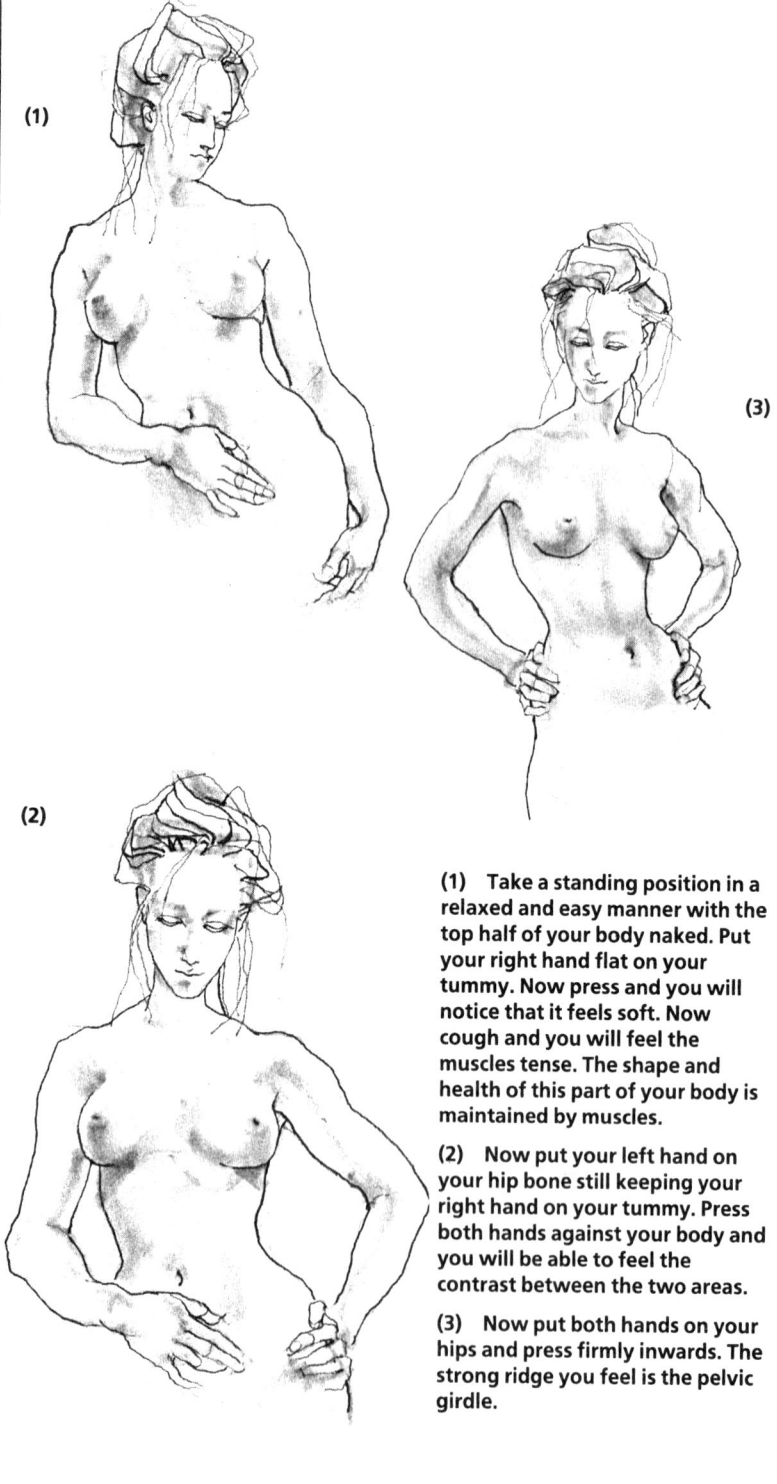

(1)

(3)

(2)

(1)   Take a standing position in a relaxed and easy manner with the top half of your body naked. Put your right hand flat on your tummy. Now press and you will notice that it feels soft. Now cough and you will feel the muscles tense. The shape and health of this part of your body is maintained by muscles.

(2)   Now put your left hand on your hip bone still keeping your right hand on your tummy. Press both hands against your body and you will be able to feel the contrast between the two areas.

(3)   Now put both hands on your hips and press firmly inwards. The strong ridge you feel is the pelvic girdle.

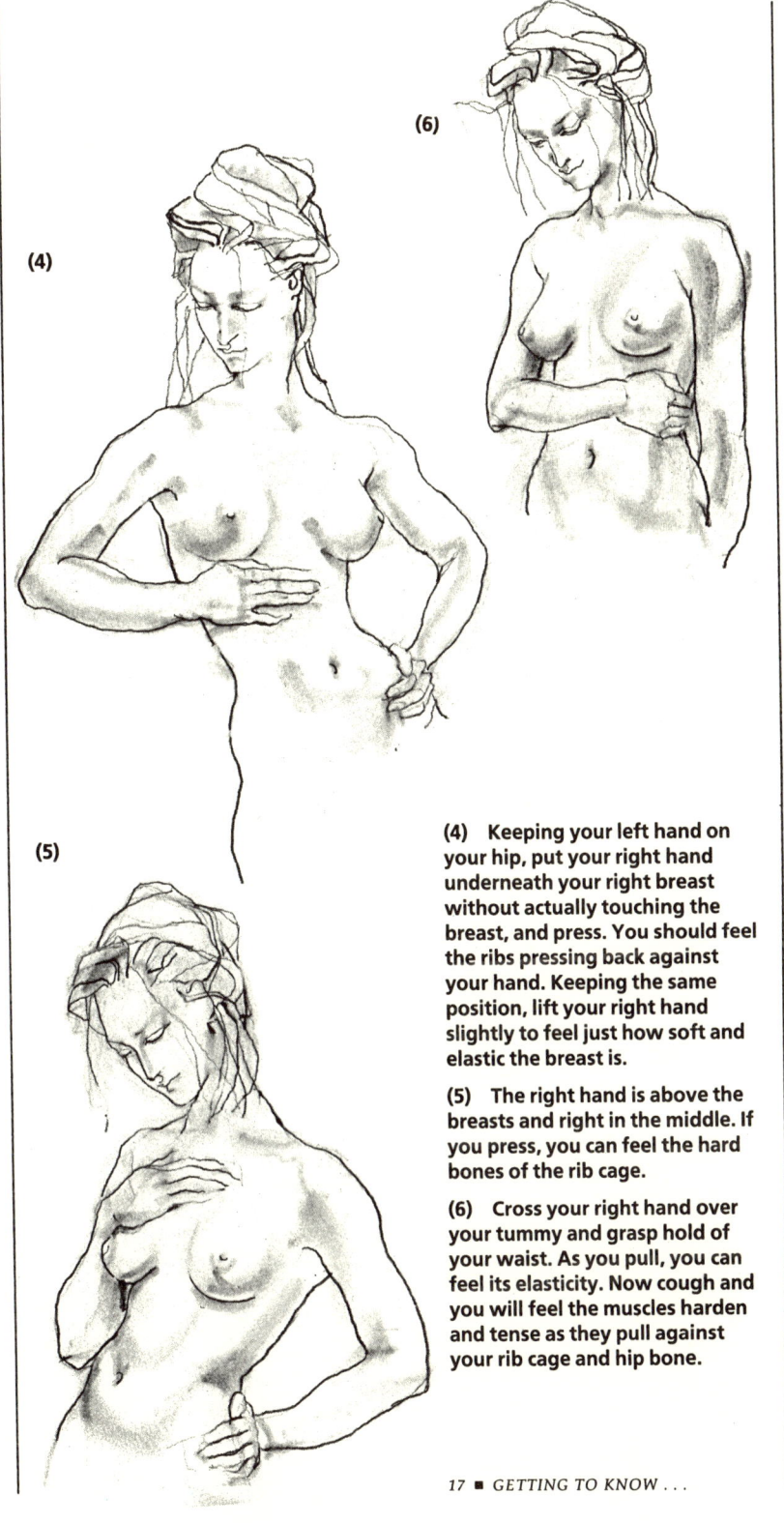

(4)   Keeping your left hand on your hip, put your right hand underneath your right breast without actually touching the breast, and press. You should feel the ribs pressing back against your hand. Keeping the same position, lift your right hand slightly to feel just how soft and elastic the breast is.

(5)   The right hand is above the breasts and right in the middle. If you press, you can feel the hard bones of the rib cage.

(6)   Cross your right hand over your tummy and grasp hold of your waist. As you pull, you can feel its elasticity. Now cough and you will feel the muscles harden and tense as they pull against your rib cage and hip bone.

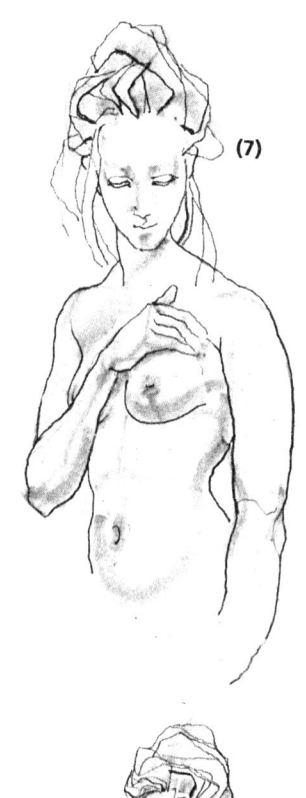

(7)

(8)

(9)

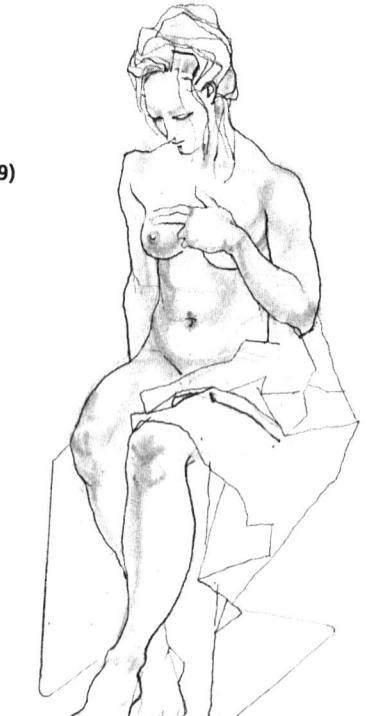

(7) Again using your right hand, put your hand over on your left breast and grasp gently. You can feel that the tissue is soft and spongy. Now cough and you will find that it makes very little difference, showing that there are very few muscles actually in the breast itself.

(8) Put your hands behind your head and really stretch back. You can see how your breasts are positioned on your rib cage.

In order to understand the construction of your breasts, soft structures which contain no bones and only a small amount of muscle tissue, follow these steps:
(9) Sit on a chair in a relaxed easy position. Press the upper part of the breast against the rib cage with your first two fingers. If you move your fingers back and forth, you will feel how the breast varies in texture under your fingers. You will be able to feel the beginning of milk tubules.

(10)

(11)

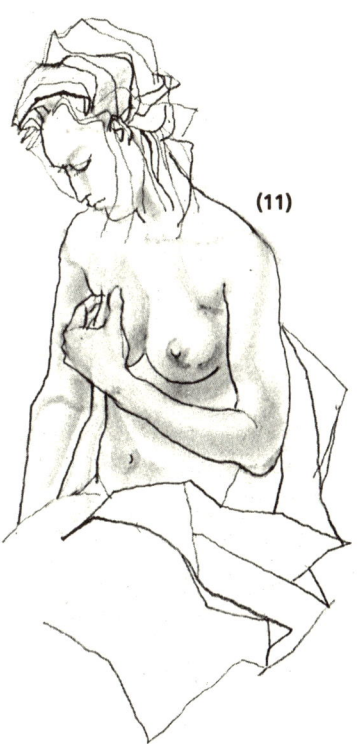

(12)

(10) Put your left hand under your right armpit, gently placing the fingers deep into the armpit. Gently move your fingertips around. You will feel the soft tissue and the lymphatic ducts.

(11) Pinch the top of your breast and pull out the thinnest possible pinch of skin. This will show you how thick your skin is here. In a young woman, this is usually about ½" thick, though in an obese young woman, it can go up to 1½" or even more. In older women, the skin usually comes away from the fat layer and often feels very thin.

(12) If you hold the breast up and take a deep pinch, as opposed to just pinching the skin, you will be able to feel the milk glands again as you move your finger and thumb together over the tissue.

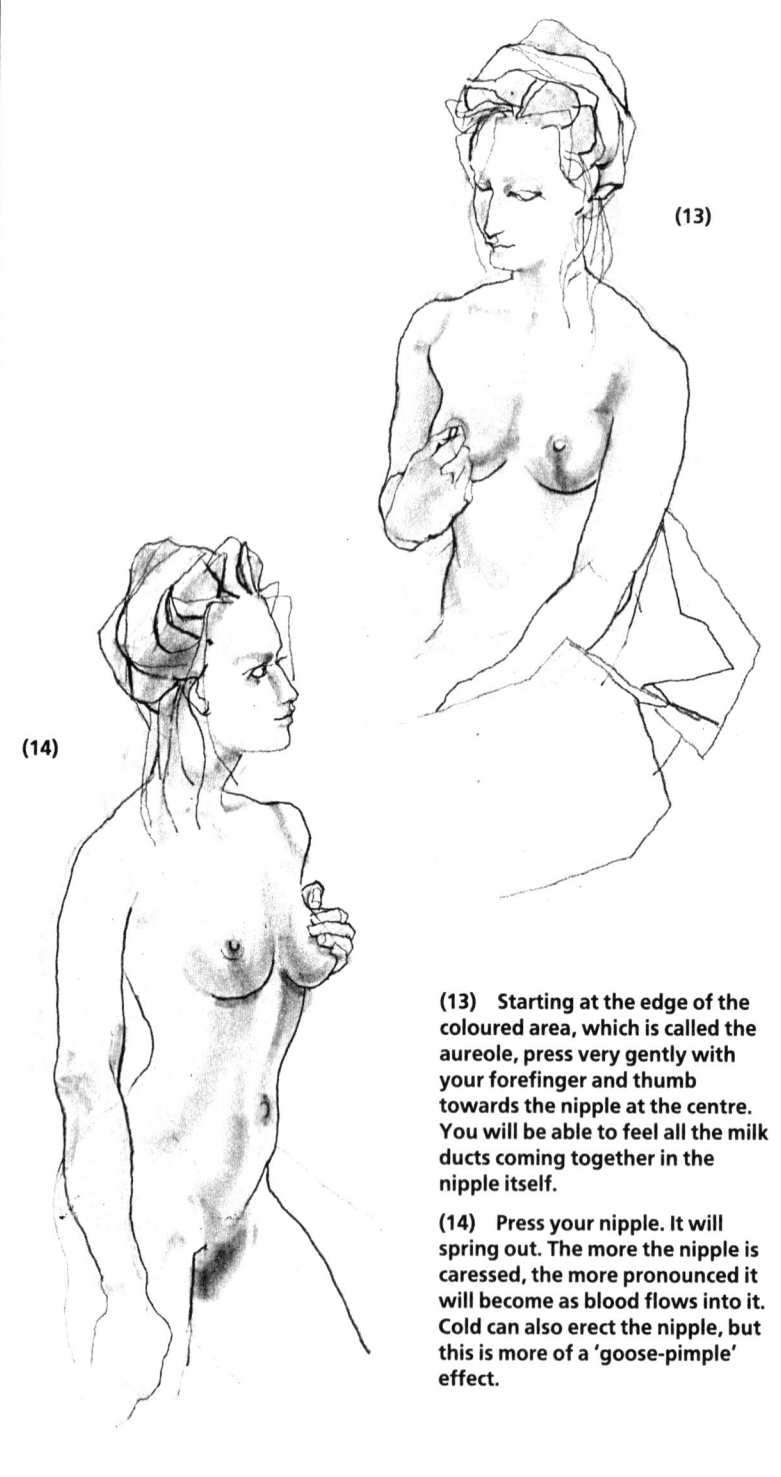

(13)

(14)

(13) Starting at the edge of the coloured area, which is called the aureole, press very gently with your forefinger and thumb towards the nipple at the centre. You will be able to feel all the milk ducts coming together in the nipple itself.

(14) Press your nipple. It will spring out. The more the nipple is caressed, the more pronounced it will become as blood flows into it. Cold can also erect the nipple, but this is more of a 'goose-pimple' effect.

3. MUSCLES, STRESS AND TENSION

Even when a muscle is not being used it quivers, slightly contracting and then relaxing. When you are very healthy, this automatic process gives you a vibrant look and a feeling of well-being. All the muscles just under the skin are under conscious control, a fact tht is exploited in Sexual Exercises. There are however many deeper muscles inside your body, which are not normally under your conscious control, but which are often rigid through bad habits and stress. This stops the natural flow of pleasure through parts of the body, particularly in the pelvic floor. Sexual Exercises can help you experience the feelings in these muscles and in time, you will be able to relax and contract them naturally, instead of their being unconsciously tense through anxiety and stress.

Here are some very simple demonstrtions to show how intimately related muscles and feelings are. Twist your head from side to side; this usually produces tension which is then dissipated when you let your head fall gently and breathe out.

Tightening or clenching your buttocks builds sexual excitement. When the buttocks are relaxed, there is an immediate flow of sexual energy.

Stand with your legs apart and your arms above your head. Breathe in and tighten your buttocks. Exhale with a deep sigh and squat down on to your haunches. Feel the rush of sexual warmth up your tummy and down your thighs from deep inside your vagina. If your buttocks are always clenched, you are suffering from sexual tension.

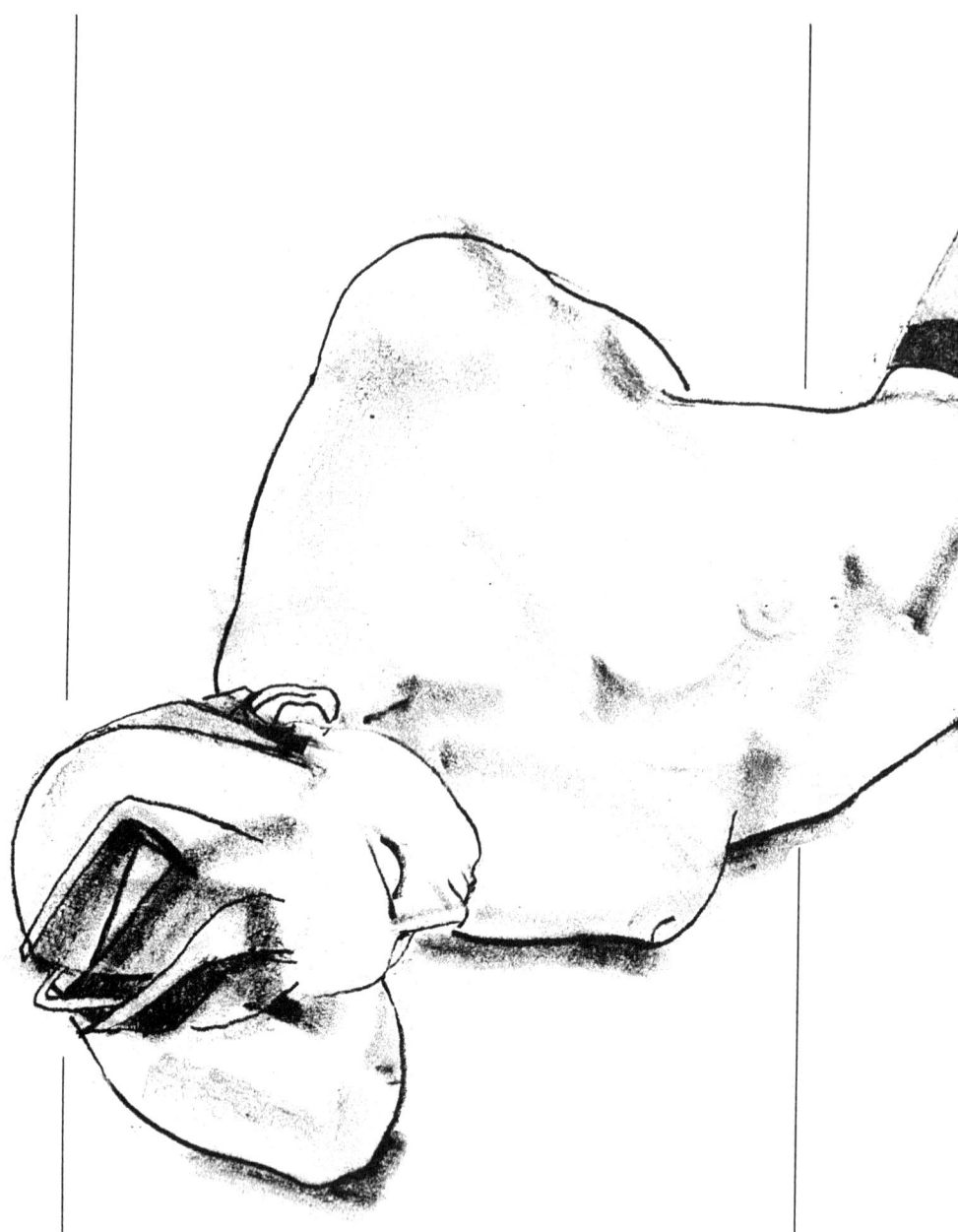

4. INTERNAL STRUCTURE

PELVIC GIRDLE, PELVIC FLOOR, PC MUSCLE Most people have very little idea how they are made and which parts of the body serve what function. Even those who can identify

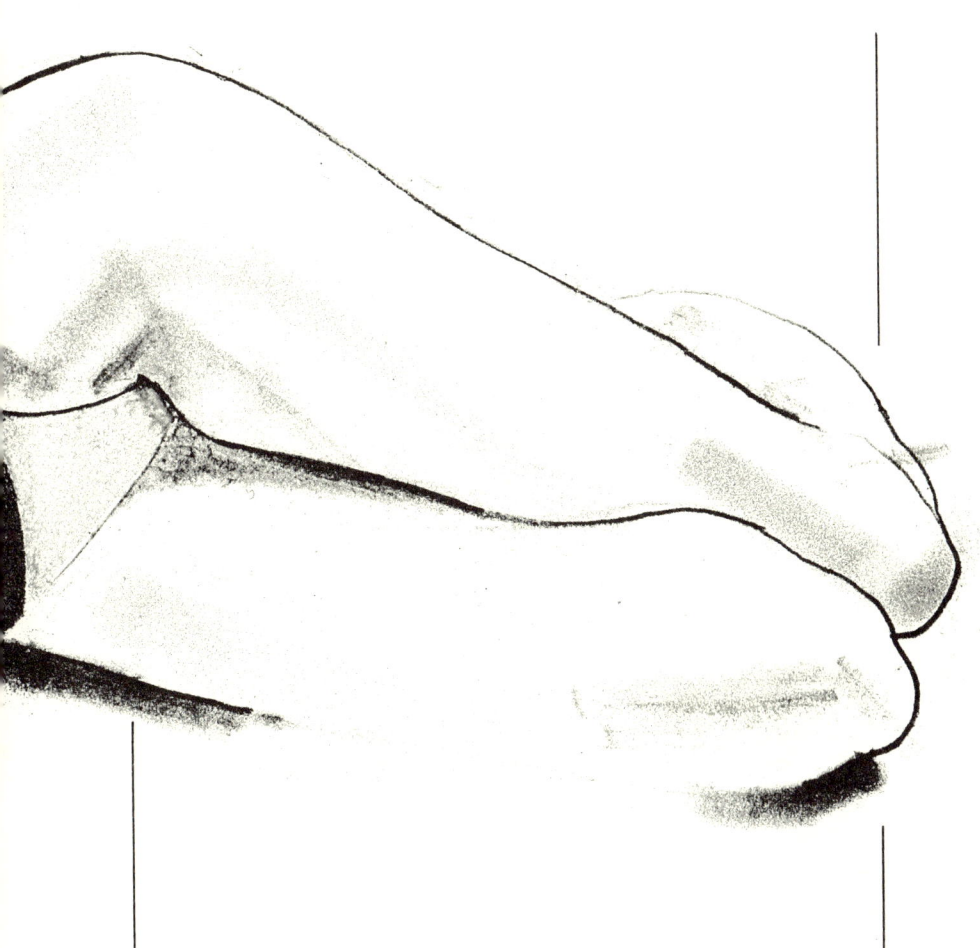

the various organs on a diagram often have difficulty locating them on themselves. Your basic shape is dictated by your bones, but it is your muscles which retain the shape and keep it smooth. Your skin, with its layer of subcutaneous fat, adds the final feminine line. Your breasts are a special development of the skin but their shape is also dependent on the muscles which support them.

Sexual energy, which flows within the fluids and soft tissues of the body, rests upon a solid foundation of living bone. Exercise is a prime factor in maintaining the health of the bones of the skeleton. The pull of the muscles stimulates their activity. In order to appreciate what happens when you do Sexual Exercises, it helps to have a real understanding of your skeleton.

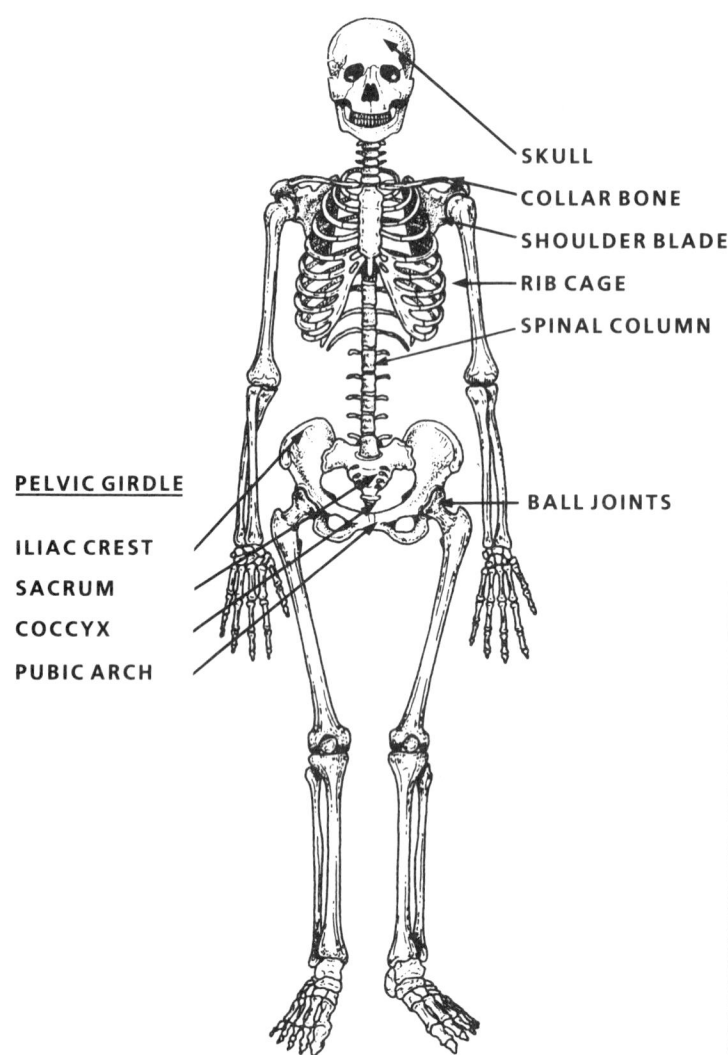

SKULL

COLLAR BONE

SHOULDER BLADE

RIB CAGE

SPINAL COLUMN

PELVIC GIRDLE

ILIAC CREST

SACRUM

COCCYX

PUBIC ARCH

BALL JOINTS

The *spinal column* runs between the *sacrum* and the *skull*. At the top end of the column, there is a simple peg joint on which the skull rests.

The barrel-shaped *rib cage* encases the heart and lungs while the *pelvic girdle* encompasses the intestines and sexual and reproductive organs, which rest on a muscular cradle, the pelvic floor.

The spine, being formed of individual bones, is very flexible. It can bend forwards and, to a more limited extent, backwards. Sexual Exercises are useful for sufferers from back pain, which is often caused by tension and stress.

The *legs* are attached to the pelvic girdle by large *ball joints*. These joints allow the thighs to rotate in a complete circle and in almost all directions of the compass, a fact which has great significance for Sexual Exercises, not only because this sophisticated system needs movement to keep it fit and healthy, but also because the inner stimulation of the tissues releases and encourages the flow of sexual energy.

The arms are attached to the skeleton via the pectoral girdle, which, unlike the pelvic girdle, is not a complete ring, but consists of two *collar bones* and two *shoulder blades*, held in place by tendons. Though the tissues of the pectoral girdle have nothing like the nervous supply and sexual potential of those of the pelvic girdle, it is important to realize that sexual tension and malaise can reveal themselves through the muscles of this girdle. A humped and rigid back and knotted muscles are just a few of the signs of tension. The Cockney expression 'she has the hump' eloquently combines the observation that bad temper and irritability are often accompanied by a tensing of the back and shoulders.

PELVIC GIRDLE   The *pelvic girdle*, which is so clearly indicated in women by the width of the hips, also surrounds the region where many sexual feelings are experienced. Many women are not aware of having a pelvic girdle, but are aware of their hips, small of the back, and the smoothly jutting curve of their bodies beneath the pubic hair, the pubic bone. We can think of the pelvic girdle as a hoop, though it is in fact, composed of several bones. You can feel the *iliac crest* (hip bone) when you stand with arms akimbo, and the arch or mound beneath your pubic hair is the *pubic arch*. If you lie on your back, your hip bones stick out, and if you are slim and in good muscle tone, the pubic bone curves up from the belly. (This is so obvious in many women it has been called the *mons veneris* or mountain of Venus.) Between your buttocks you can gently feel your *coccyx*, while the strong foundation of the lower back is the *sacrum*, which is formed by the fused individual *vertebrae* of the spinal column.

The pelvic girdle has a hole in its centre, which is filled in by several very important sheaths of muscle, which form an elastic support to the soft organs of the abdomen. This pelvic floor is of crucial importance to health.

PELVIC FLOOR   The sheath of muscle covering the hole of the pelvic girdle has various holes through it: the anus, the vagina, and the urinary tube from the bladder, as well as numerous nerves, veins, arteries and lymph tubes.

In healthy women there is considerable control over this pelvic floor, so that they can contract the whole, or part of it, for ease of urination, or retention of urination, for opening and shutting the vagina, and bringing pressure to bear or releasing it on the vaginal walls.

Although we call it floor, it is not flat, but curves up at the front to meet the *mons veneris*.

PC MUSCLE   Recently in a spate of books the retention of urine has been ascribed solely to the PC (pubococcygeus) muscle. It is part of the pelvic floor, but it is unlikely only this muscle is involved, since there are so many in the pelvic floor.

5. PRE-MENSTRUAL TENSION AND MENSTRUATION

In any discussion of female sexuality and physiology, it would be difficult and ill-advised to ignore the menstrual cycle. In recent years, much has been made of pre-menstrual tension and its effects on day-to-day living. Given that Sexual Exercises are designed to increase your awareness of your own body and improve its condition and responses, it is hardly surprising that the exercises have been found to have a beneficial effect, not just on the cramps experienced during menstruation, but also on the tensions, both physical and mental, associated with the pre-menstrual period.

PHYSICAL SYMPTOMS

SWELLING: Many women complain of feeling bloated just before their period. This is because the hormonal changes induced by and inducing menstruation upset the balance of water and salts in the tissues, and cause fluids to collect, so joints and breasts swell. The breasts often feel tender.

WEIGHT GAIN: This is related to swelling and is caused by water retention. It is not unusual for a woman to gain as much as 5lbs at this point in the cycle but there is no need to diet as this is not a genuine weight gain.

HEADACHES: These are a symptom of tension and can be very unpleasant as sufferers find that they tend to get worse as the period comes on. Cramps during actual menstruation can cause tension in the back and neck, which in turn creates a headache.

CONSTIPATION OR DIARRHOEA: The former is often caused by water being drained off from the faeces in the rectum, making them too hard for evacuation; the latter by insufficient water being drained off. These phenomena are clearly related to the same set of fluid-regulating hormones whose imbalance results in swelling.

CLUMSINESS: To be precise, a deterioration of the motor and timing ability. In other words, you drop things you normally would not. This is a real phenomenon and not within your control. If you are suffering from pre-menstrual tension and clumsiness is one of the symptoms, you should avoid driving cars, using delicate instruments or indeed performing any act requiring more than normal levels of physical control and dexterity.

INSOMNIA: This is a classic response to stress.

Along with the above symptoms, others frequently reported are unusual food cravings, vomiting, and of course, discomfort from the menstrual cramps.

MENTAL SYMPTOMS

DEPRESSION: Moods are cyclic in even the most level-headed person, male or female. Depression, however unpleasant, appears to be a natural state for short periods of time. Experience teaches us not to trust the judgements and responses we have during depression. If, however, your depression appears to be chronic, you may benefit from medical help.

LETHARGY: This often occurs both during the pre-menstrual period and during menstruation itself, particularly if you suffer from painful periods. Mild fatigue is part of menstruation but not all women experience it.

ANGER: By this is meant inappropriate anger, or irritability to such a degree that balanced trustworthy reactions are no longer possible. This indicates severe stress, and you should attempt to avoid trying and testing situations. However, many women cannot escape trying circumstances, especially if they have children, jobs and families. The first step is to recognize that when your next period comes, you will face the same problems again. Try to find some way of planning ahead.

ANXIETY: This means worry without due cause, and, as such, is a sign of stress. If it comes on with your period or its approach, you need to treat it like anger (see above); you need to realize that your emotional and mental climate are so changed by the biochemical alterations in your body, and your brain, that you literally cannot cope, at least, not until you have learned to live with your 'new personality'.

The obvious response to such a disconcerting catalogue of aches and pains is to wonder why a natural function like menstruation should cause so many problems. Many women actually find no difficulty, so there is no easy answer to this, and it is therefore far more helpful and constructive to look at ways of dealing with the problem.

Sexual Exercises appear to reduce the severity of the cramps, and in that they can lead you to a deeper understanding of your body and its needs, weaknesses and strengths, they should help you to start seeing more clearly the ways in which you need to develop and change, both physically and mentally. As you increase your knowledge of yourself, so you build up your resistance to stress, and eventually menstruation should become simply one more natural function.

The cramps are helped by the following exercises: squatting, quivering, arching and cooling. If you suffer from PMT, the trouble is more deep-rooted and you must not expect rapid solutions. A patient, careful, gentle increase in your personal and sexual awareness over several months is the most rewarding approach.

PART TWO: GENERAL EXERCISES

The fitter your body becomes, the more easy and powerful your sexual response will be. Equally, the better you are able to mobilize your own sexual energies, the healthier you will be.

Many women can turn straight away to the exercises described in Part Three and derive great benefit and improvement from them. Others will find that Part Two is a better way to start, particularly if they feel that they are very unfit and have not been anything but sedentary for a long period.

The work in this section should be returned to from time to time, even if you have become very expert at Sexual Exercises.

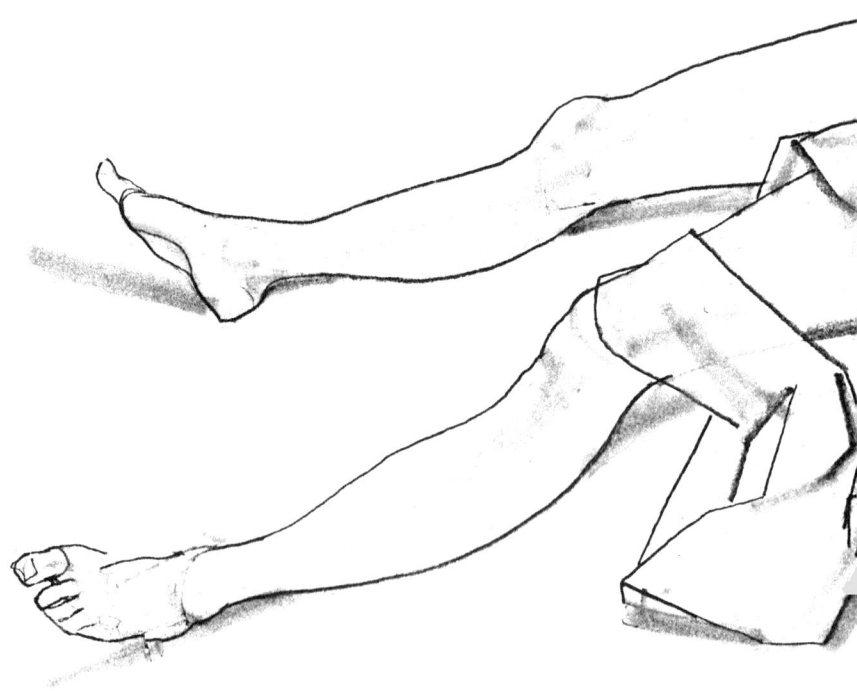

1. GETTING IN TOUCH WITH YOUR BODY

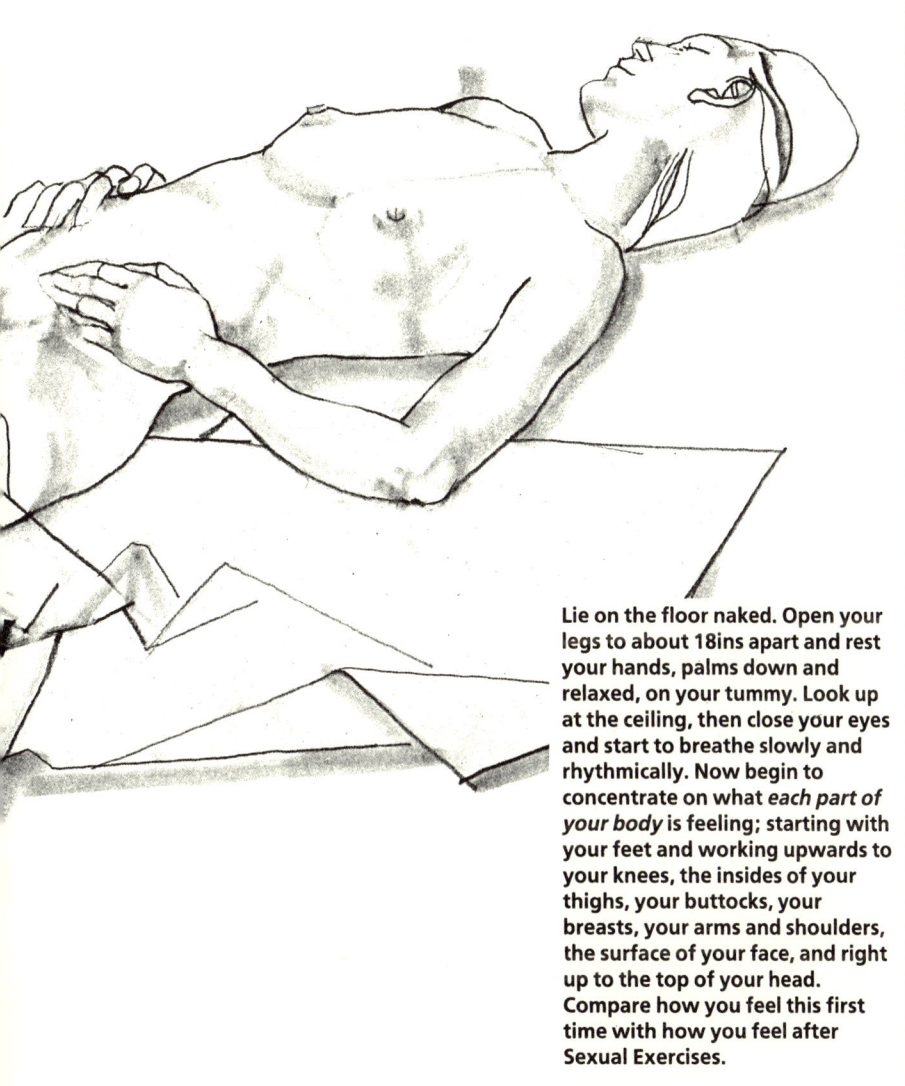

Lie on the floor naked. Open your legs to about 18ins apart and rest your hands, palms down and relaxed, on your tummy. Look up at the ceiling, then close your eyes and start to breathe slowly and rhythmically. Now begin to concentrate on what *each part of your body* is feeling; starting with your feet and working upwards to your knees, the insides of your thighs, your buttocks, your breasts, your arms and shoulders, the surface of your face, and right up to the top of your head. Compare how you feel this first time with how you feel after Sexual Exercises.

2. WORK-OUTS

These movements are for basic strengthening and toning of the body. Exercise in a warm, draught-free room on a thick rug, carpet or thin mattress. Wear either loose clothing or none at all. When resting between exercises, put on a robe. Do not get cold. Do not attempt these schedules within an hour before a meal or two hours after a meal. Some people find that when the schedules are performed just before bed they induce immediate relaxed sleep. After a schedule, rest for five or ten minutes, but make sure you do not get cold. These exercises are quite strenuous and are therefore not intended to be done every day. It is not advisable to do them more than three times a week and never on two consecutive days. Most women will find that twice a week is ample. Do not attempt them if you are pregnant. They can show you what you can aspire to, but you may like to try others first, for instance suppleness and stretching.

WAIST
Lie on your back with your hands firmly placed palms down by your sides. Raise your legs and reach back with them to touch the ground behind your head (1), then flick them quickly forward *stopping them about a foot from the floor.* Lower them gently and then start the exercise over again. You may find you have to open your legs to do so. When you flick your legs forward, you will have to push hard on your hands to stop the descent of your legs. Keep your head down. This exercise is a very fine shaper of the tummy.

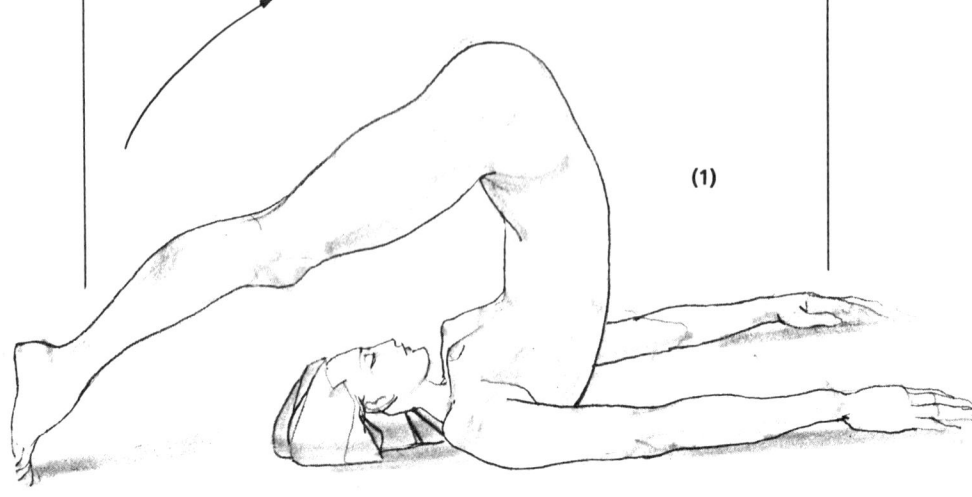

(1)

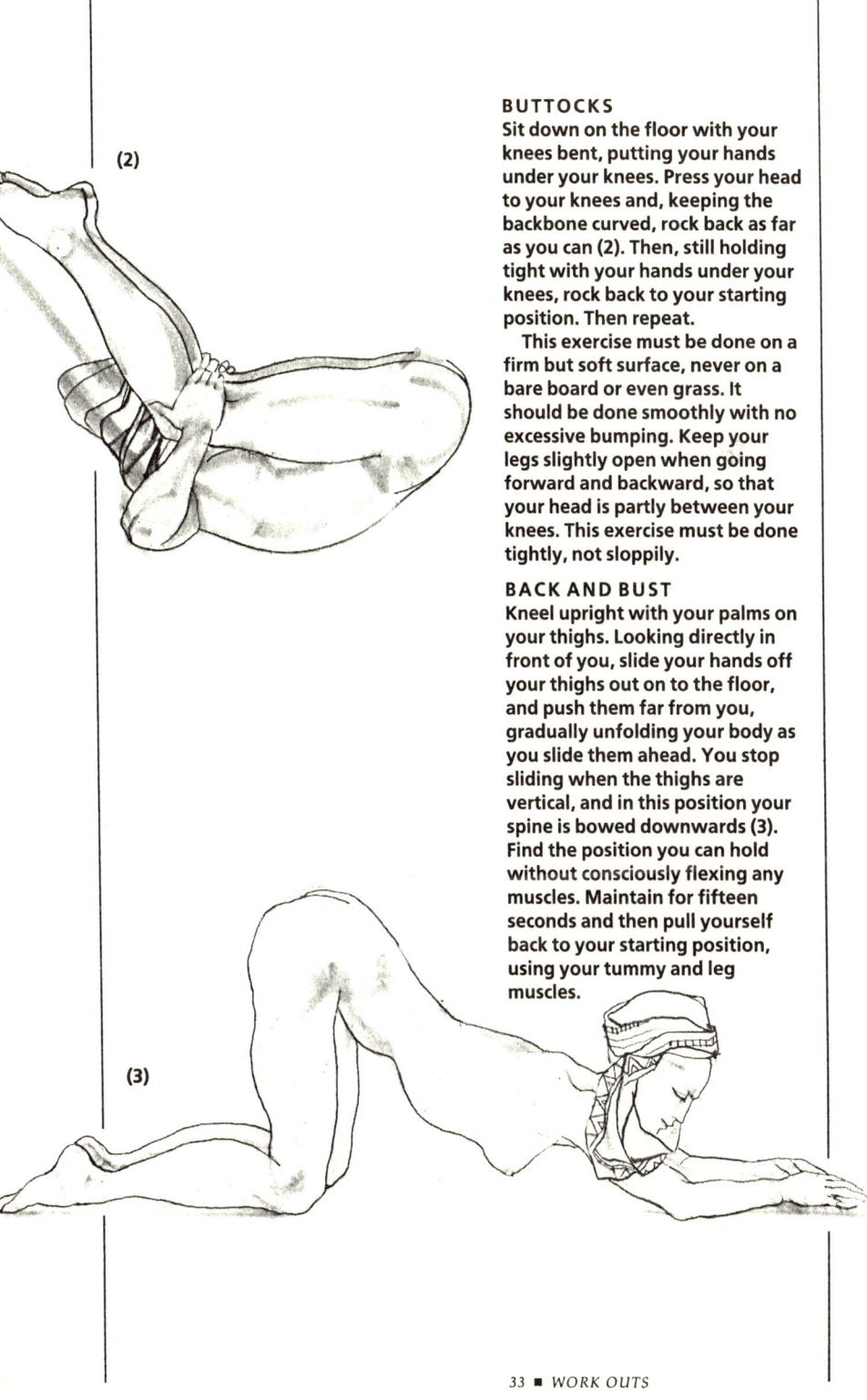

(2)

BUTTOCKS

Sit down on the floor with your knees bent, putting your hands under your knees. Press your head to your knees and, keeping the backbone curved, rock back as far as you can (2). Then, still holding tight with your hands under your knees, rock back to your starting position. Then repeat.

This exercise must be done on a firm but soft surface, never on a bare board or even grass. It should be done smoothly with no excessive bumping. Keep your legs slightly open when going forward and backward, so that your head is partly between your knees. This exercise must be done tightly, not sloppily.

BACK AND BUST

Kneel upright with your palms on your thighs. Looking directly in front of you, slide your hands off your thighs out on to the floor, and push them far from you, gradually unfolding your body as you slide them ahead. You stop sliding when the thighs are vertical, and in this position your spine is bowed downwards (3). Find the position you can hold without consciously flexing any muscles. Maintain for fifteen seconds and then pull yourself back to your starting position, using your tummy and leg muscles.

(3)

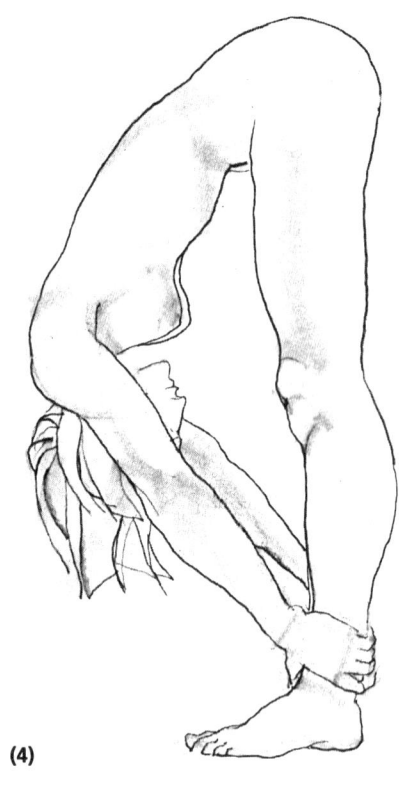

(4)

BUST AND SHOULDERS

Stand with your legs about 18ins apart and grasp your ankles (4). Breathe in, pull on your legs and pull your tummy in. Hold for fifteen seconds. Caution: do this gently at first.

THIGHS AND CROTCH

Sit on the floor with your legs straight out in front of you. Put your hands behind you, resting the weight of your back upon your hands with your fingers pointing in the opposite direction to your legs. Now raise your whole body up on your toes forming a bridge. Let your head hang (5). From this position, push your pubic arch as high as you possibly can and then let it relax, so that you almost touch the ground, and then push back up again.

This exercise can be done properly only if the palms of the hands form a support, and the shin bones are vertical when you are in the bridge position. It is also quite important to have your legs wide apart, about 18ins to 2ft, so that there is just a slight discomfort in the width of the spread which you then reduce until it is comfortable.

SCHEDULES	I	II	III
Waist	3 × 10	3 × 9	4 × 3
Buttocks	3 × 7	4 × 5	4 × 4
Back and Bust	4 × 4	5 × 3	3 × 3
Bust and shoulders	5 × 8	7 × 5	8 × 1
Thigh and Crotch	3 × 10	3 × 8	4 × 4

4 × 7 means perform the exercise continuously seven times, then rest till you feel ready to attempt it again (one or two minutes) and perform another seven times, then rest, and so on, until you have completed the cycle four times. Rest between each different exercise, till you feel ready to continue.

HOW TO USE THE SCHEDULES

If you haven't done any exercise, or you are over twenty-one, start at III for one week and *gradually* work through II to I. Do not get disheartened, do the work gently not harshly. If you are fat, but otherwise fit, start at III for one week, then move on to II in the second week, and only move on to I when you feel comfortable. If you really are fit, try I but do so gently (you may not be as fit as you think).

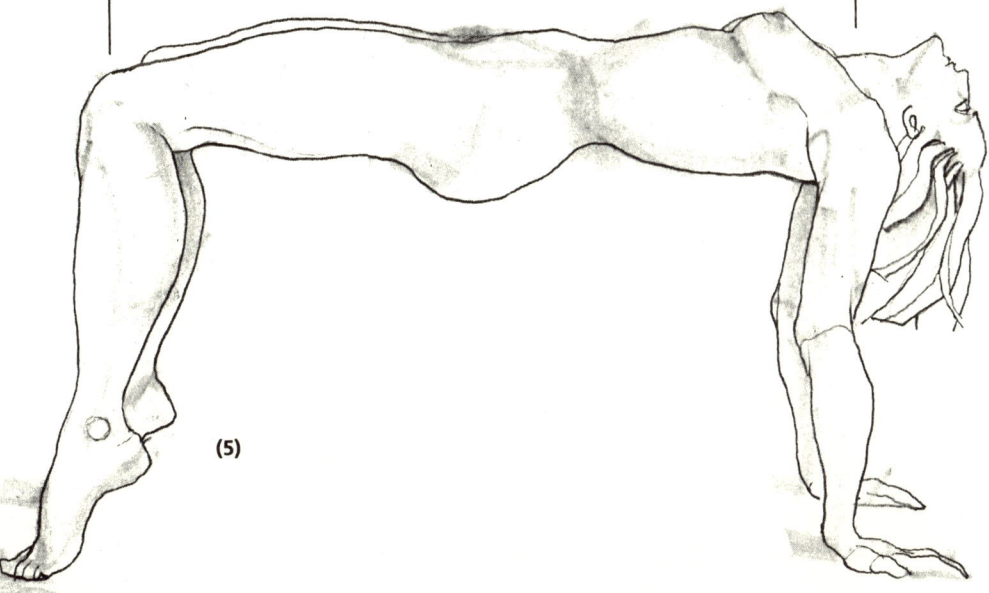

(5)

3. STRETCHING

Tension occurs when the muscles are contracted to no purpose, but if the tension is not chronic, it can be released by deliberately increasing it in certain areas. The argument behind this is that if you deliberately increase muscular contraction in a specific area, you reach a point of maximum tension, and when you relax, the residual tension is dissipated at the same time. The following sequence of exercises is particularly effective for this.

Exercise in a warm room, wearing either comfortable loose clothing or none at all. Do the movements lying on a large pouffe if you have one, or on a pile of large cushions. It is a good idea to take a shower or bath afterwards.

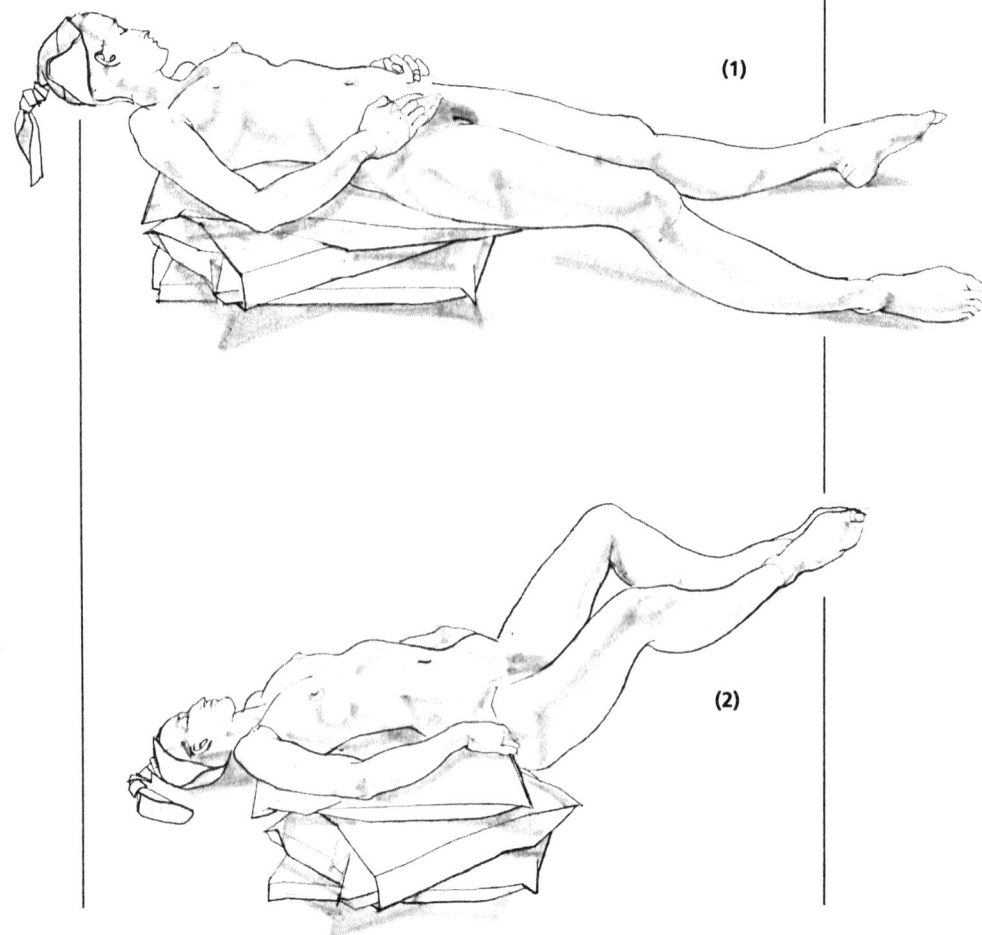

(1)

(2)

VENTRAL STRETCHING

Lie on your back with your legs gently but fully stretched out, and press your hands on your hip bones. As you breathe in to a count of four, press your heels down on the floor (1). Then exhale to a count of five and gradually relax your body. Repeat this cycle three times.

As you come to the end of the last cycle, breathe in and raise your knees, putting your hands by your sides (2).

Breathe out and drop your legs to floor, still bent at the knees, and lower your head (3). Breathe in on a count of three to return to position (1), pressing the soles of your feet together, and then breathing out on a count of five, relax back into position (3). Repeat this cycle three times.

(3)

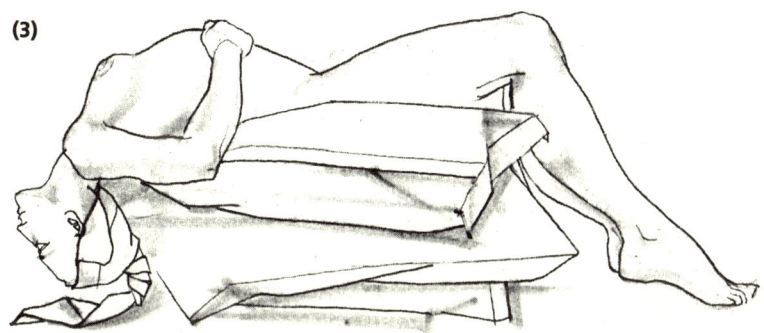

Basic ventral stretching takes between five and six minutes, although cumulative effects can be achieved by prolonging the work. Do it just before going to bed or when you are feeling tense.

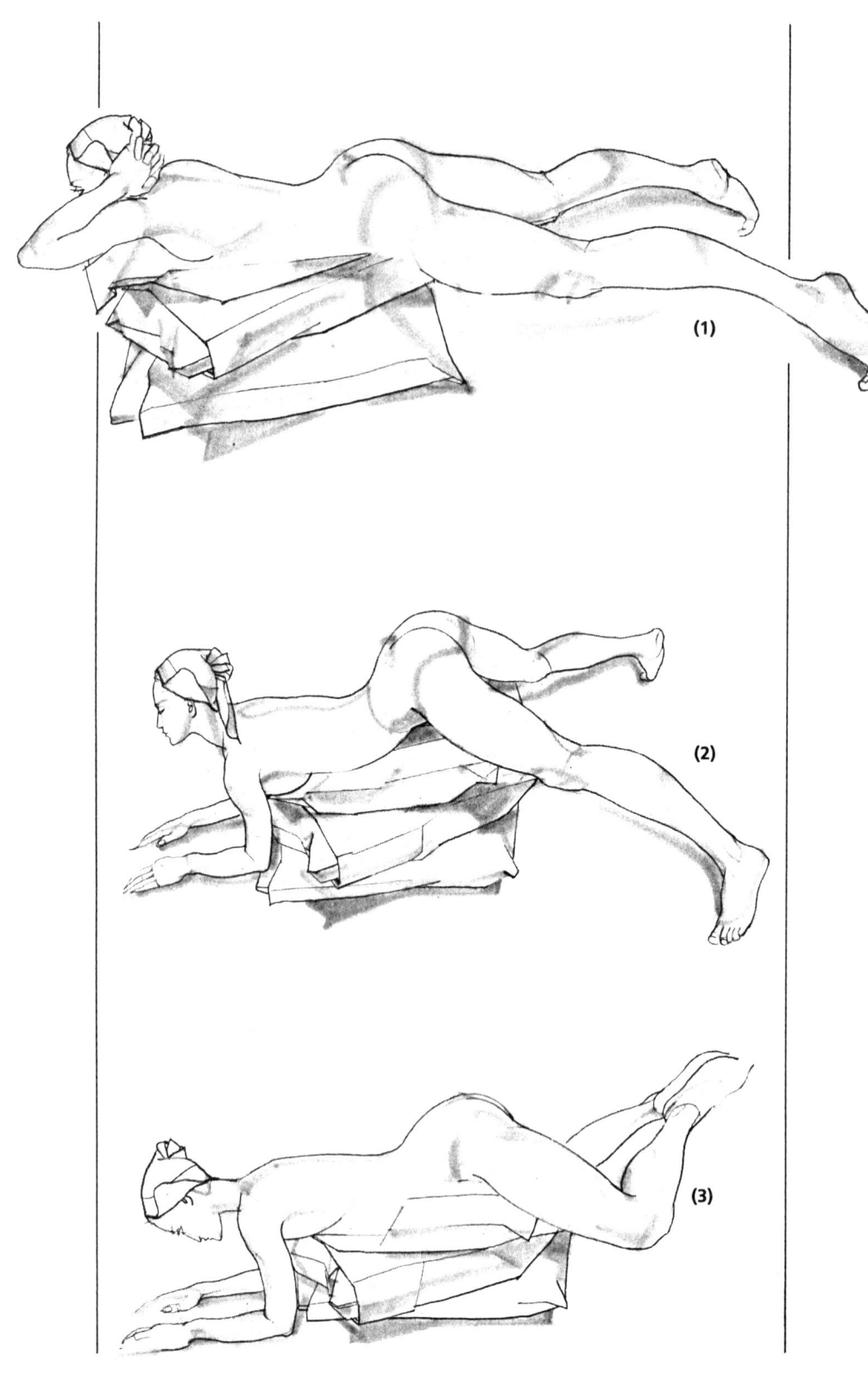

(1)

(2)

(3)

DORSAL STRETCHING

Lie on your tummy with your legs apart and your hands clasped behind your neck (1). Tense your body by lifting your feet from the floor as you breathe in for a count of three.

Exhale from the previous position as you move to raise your buttocks and place your elbows on the floor with your forearms lying flat (2). Repeat this cycle (from (1) to (2) and back again) three times.

Keep your arms in the same position, lift your legs bringing your heels up towards your buttocks.

Then, bring the soles of your feet together with increasing pressure, breathing in as you do so to a count of four (3). Hold for a count of two and then relax back into position (2) while you count five. Relax your buttocks.

Repeat this cycle (from (2) to (3) and back again) six times.

After stretching, if you lie as shown in the illustration (4) you will find a little pleasurable flow along the straight leg, but warmth on the bent leg, which increases the more you bring it up towards your tummy.

(4)

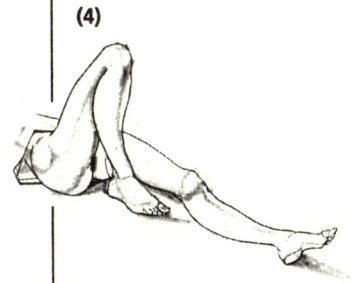

4. ENERGIZING

This exercise is an all-round tension reducer and is especially effective in relieving tense feelings in the throat. Once that has been achieved, further practice of the exercise will energize you.

When you are tired, your tummy sags or your spine curves. But when you are feeling energetic, your tummy muscles are taut, but not tense, and your spine is supple. Imagine a line running down from your throat between your breasts over your tummy and navel, down to your crotch and up through the cleft of your buttocks along your backbone to your neck. This is a primary energy line.

When the muscles running either side of this line are in good tune, you feel fit, healthy and full of energy.

(1)

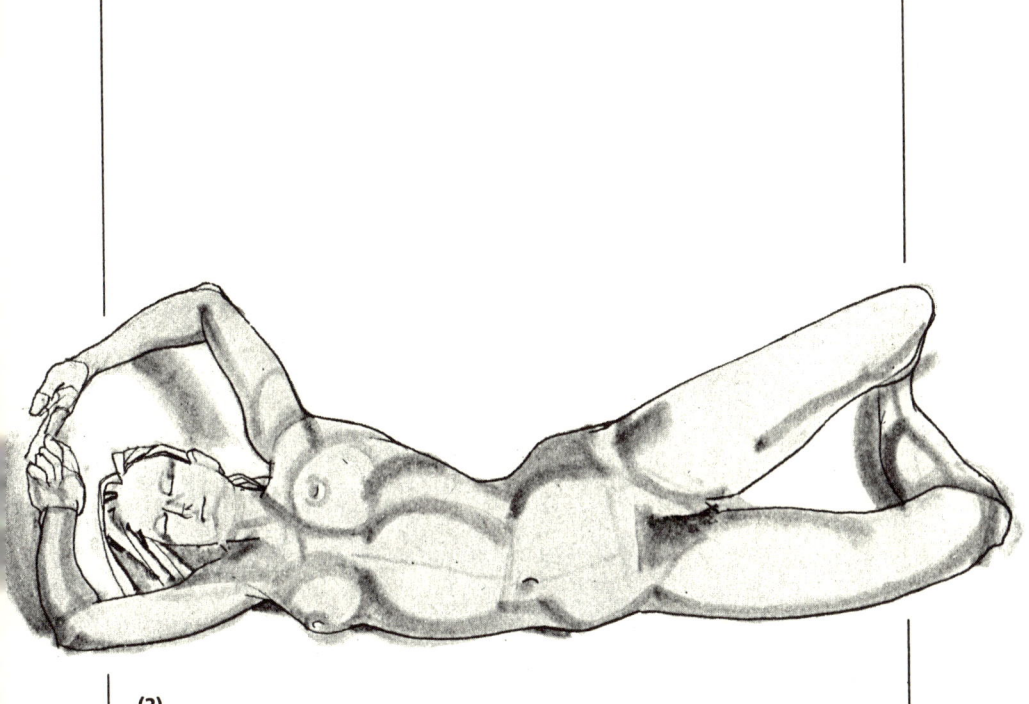

(2)

To energize your body bilaterally
(on both sides) of the line, lie on
your side as shown (1). This
reduces tension in your back.
Breathe quietly, or even hum.
Then gradually inhale as you
smoothly stretch to the second
position (2). Hold until it becomes
uncomfortable, then exhale while
returning to the first position.
Notice how your knees are next to
one another when you start but in
the stretched position they are
apart, while the feet are still
together. This is a reflex and
shows you are moving in an
anatomically correct way with no
unnecessary tensions. Do the
exercise a few more times,
stretching gently but firmly, and
then work on your left side.

5. SUPPLENESS

SIMPLE EXERCISES

A healthy body is supple. Tension diminishes suppleness so that the spine cannot arch nor the joints move freely, which leads to poor posture, discomfort and reduced sexual ability.

These exercises stretch the spine, making you more supple. They shape the small of your back, your breasts and the tops of your thighs. Once you have mastered them, you can do them to music if you find it easier.

(1)

(2)

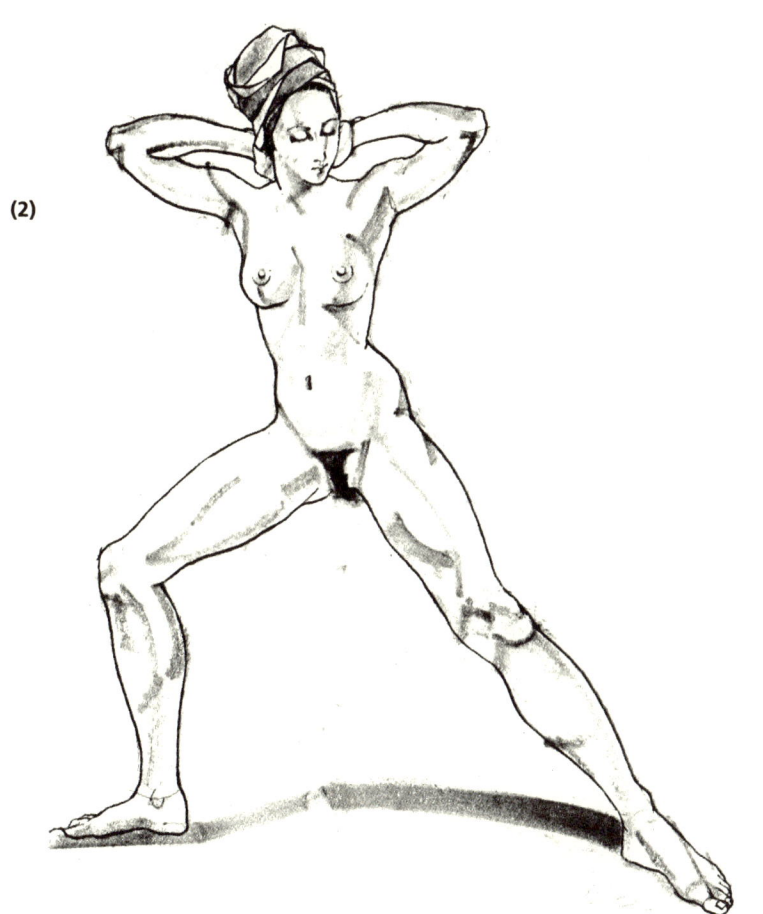

Stand erect, heels together, toes slightly apart, with hands clasped behind your head. Breathe in gently, then, as you breathe out lunge forward (1). Inhale, exhale, then, as you return to your starting position inhale again. You can repeat this up to ten times for each leg, but do it gently at first. The more you do the exercise, the more you will be able to stretch your legs.

To vary the exercise, start as above, but then, as you breathe out, step sideways to the right (2). Return to the starting position. Do this exercise ten times to each side. This is effective in shaping your hips and inner thighs.

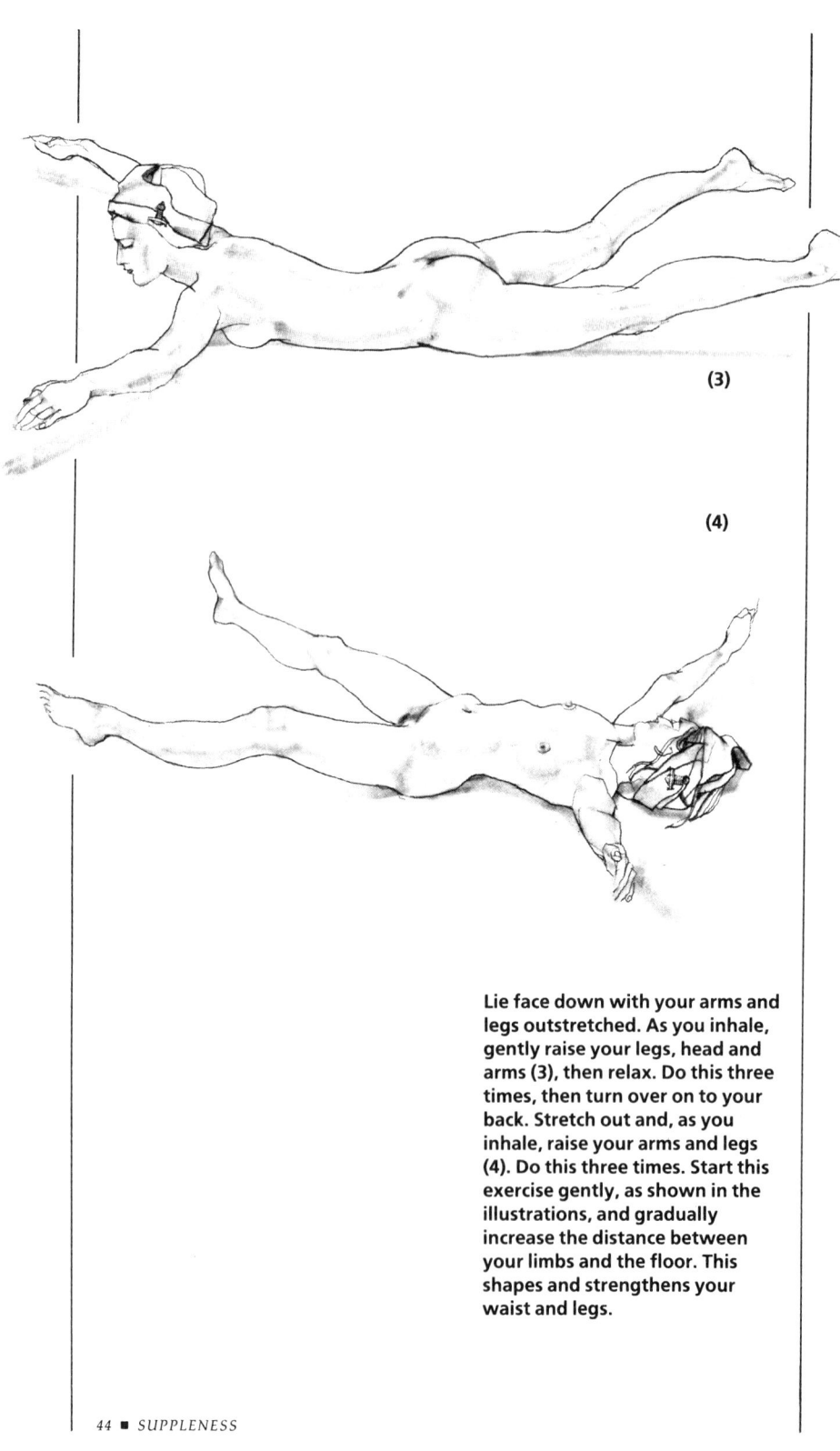

(3)

(4)

Lie face down with your arms and legs outstretched. As you inhale, gently raise your legs, head and arms (3), then relax. Do this three times, then turn over on to your back. Stretch out and, as you inhale, raise your arms and legs (4). Do this three times. Start this exercise gently, as shown in the illustrations, and gradually increase the distance between your limbs and the floor. This shapes and strengthens your waist and legs.

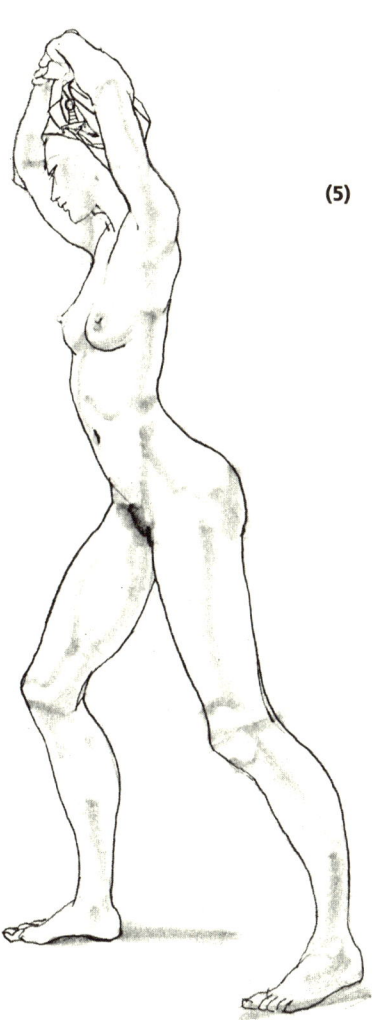

(5)

Perhaps the most graceful of the positions shown here, this is a very rejuvenating exercise which is particularly beneficial when done first thing in the morning or when you are feeling tense.

Stand erect, heels together and toes apart, with your arms at your sides. Breathing in gently, slowly raise your arms above your head and step forward simultaneously making sure that your arms curve gracefully to join above your head (5). Then, in a fluid movement, return to the starting position exhaling as you do so. When you have mastered this, take a count to five as you take up the pose (5) and count to ten as you return to your starting position. If you do this properly, you should feel very relaxed and warm.

FELIS SEQUENCE

The cat family, ranging from the domestic tabby to the cheetah and lion, has extraordinary power and grace, suppleness and control. But all cats, whether large or small, spend much of their time lying around sleeping or dozing. This is interspersed with bouts of intense activity. Observation of these beautiful creatures reveals that they exercise by stretching and relaxing, themes which run through the studies described here. Accordingly, I have called this group of exercises after the cat family.

Do all the movements smoothly and gently until you are familiar with them. Do nothing jerkily. A warm room and loose clothing are essential.

SIAMESE

Lie on the floor on your back with your arms by your sides, legs stretched out. Breathe in and out gently six times, then say to yourself: 'My feet are relaxed.' Still breathing gently throughout, say, 'my calves are relaxed', and then 'my thighs are relaxed'. Now concentrate on your arms. Work upwards from your hands saying, 'my hands are relaxed, my forearms are relaxed, my shoulders are relaxed'. Say this three times for each part of the body.

Then say four times each, concentrating on the area in question, 'my tummy is relaxed, my chest is relaxed', and, finally, 'my back is relaxed'.

Once you have run through this sequence, turn over on to your right side with your hands and feet together as shown (1). Breathe gently six times, and then, in a graceful movement, bring your feet up behind you towards your back, stretching out your hands and arching your back (2). Breathe six times in this position. Then move gently from position shown in illustration (2) to that shown in (1) by bringing your thighs towards your tummy and your hands to your chest. Breathe in and out three times in position (1) and then curl over again on to your left side, back to the starting position.

(1)

(2)

Once you have mastered the rhythm, you will find it extremely relaxing to inhale during the move from (1) to (2), and then to exhale when moving from (2) to (1). It will, however, take some time to achieve such co-ordination. Practise the simpler sequences first, making sure that you can do them while starting from your left side as described. Once you have mastered that, begin from your right side, repeating the same set of movements.

Siamese is excellent for shaping the front of your body and strengthening the small of your back.

OCELOT

Start on all fours on the floor with your palms down, your knees about a foot apart and your head facing forwards (3). Breathe in as you pull your tummy in (4). Arch your back hold the position for a count of two, then pull your tummy in. Then breathe out as you return to the starting position (3). Repeat the sequence at least six times.

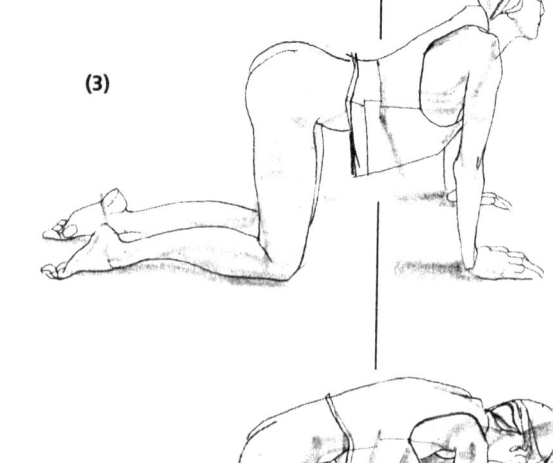

(3)

(4)

TIGER

Starting from all fours, as in Ocelot (3), breathe in as you stretch out and raise your left leg, slightly bending it at the knee as shown (5). Your leg should be lifted to its maximum height when you have fully inhaled. Hold for a count of two, then exhale naturally as you bring your leg back to starting position. Repeat six times with the left leg and then do it six times with the right leg.

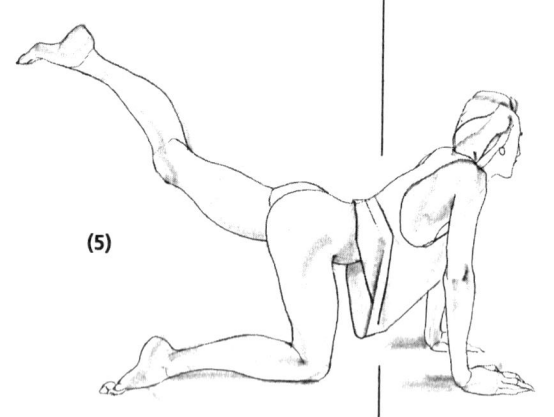

(5)

Ocelot and Tiger are both extremely relaxing exercises. They strengthen the back and also relax the too often tensed muscles of the pelvic floor. Great pleasure can be obtained through these movements, particularly once you have gone through the learning process, and have your breathing and movements exactly co-ordinated.

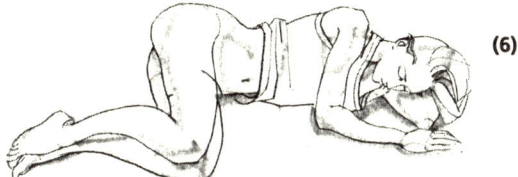

(6)

PANTHER

Lie on your left side with your knees slightly bent, your head in the crook of your left arm, and your right arm lying comfortably, with the elbow bent, in front of you (6). Very gracefully, and with maximum concentration for full control, stretch out your legs and arms so that your body makes a V shape (7), your hips being at the point of the V. Try this a few times so that you can achieve the position shown lying on your left side. Once you have mastered the movement, start again, then, as you move into the V, breathe in: The movement and the breathing should take a count of four so that by the time you reach the V position, you should have inhaled. Hold for a count of two, then breathe out as you relax into the starting position. Do this at least seven times.

This is excellent for shaping the tummy and upper thighs. It also strengthens the back. Once you have done the work on your left side, repeat the whole sequence on your right side.

(7)

6. MASSAGE

There are certain areas of the body which, when stroked, stimulate vaginal lubrication. When massaging, make sure that your nails do not scratch or cut your skin. It is often a good idea to use a moisturizing cream or oil to facilitate the massage. Apply the cream or oil in the areas marked by arrows in the drawings and then, using firm fingertip pressure, massage your skin in the direction of the arrows. If you feel any pain or discomfort, stop immediately and see your doctor. You should not massage over any kind of skin eruption, bruising or infection.

(1)

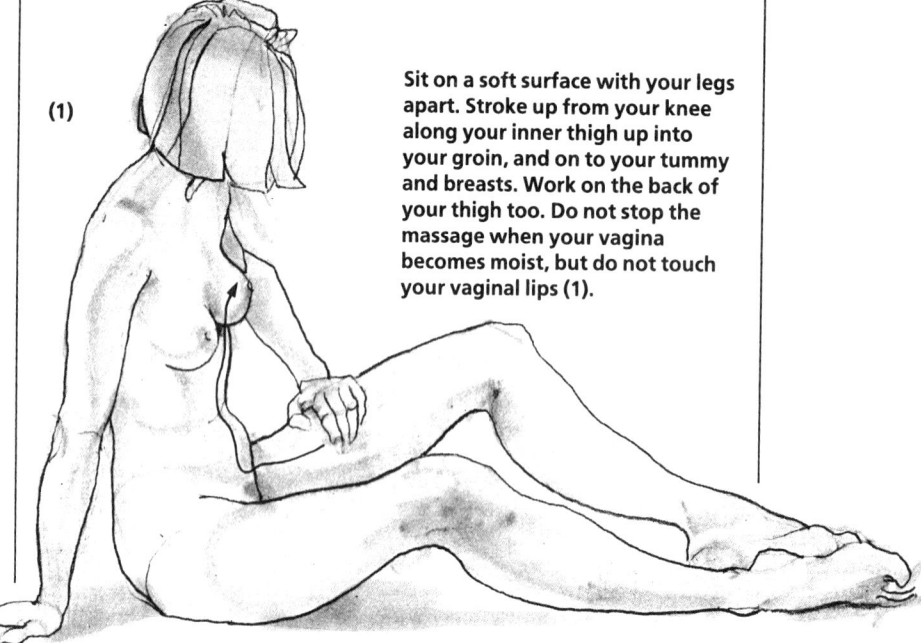

Sit on a soft surface with your legs apart. Stroke up from your knee along your inner thigh up into your groin, and on to your tummy and breasts. Work on the back of your thigh too. Do not stop the massage when your vagina becomes moist, but do not touch your vaginal lips (1).

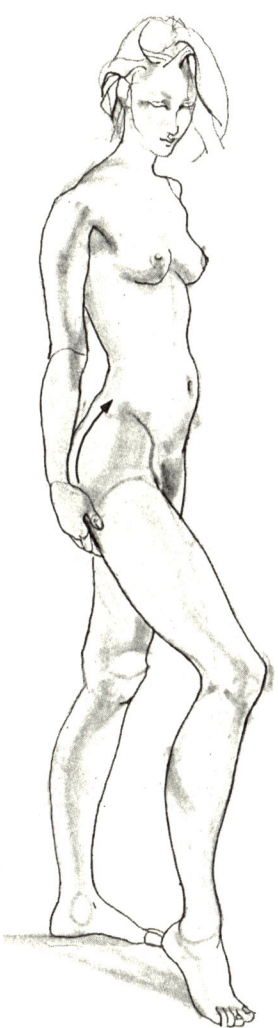

(3)

(2)

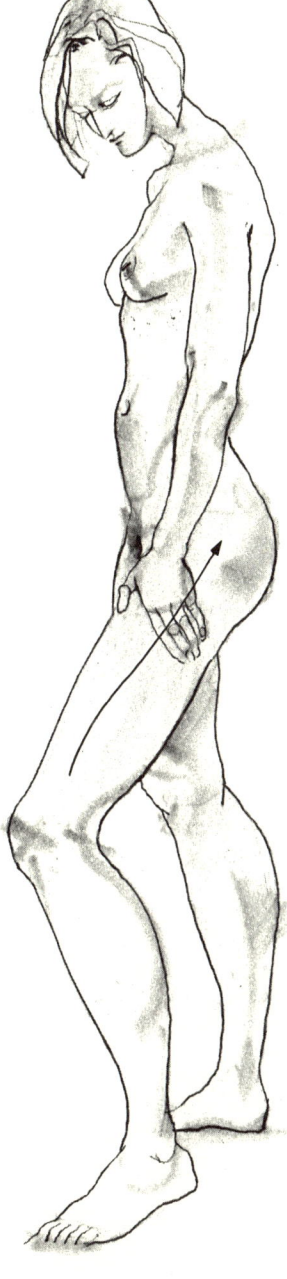

To stimulate the pleasure centres of the thighs and buttocks, stronger pressure is needed so use your whole hand rather than just your fingertips. Stand up and place your hands flat on the front of your left thigh and alternate strokes with both hands, pulling the flesh up (2). The next step (3) shows work on the buttocks, using a cupped hand to pull strongly. Note the position of the leg when it is worked on.

7. SEXUAL MERIDIA STROKING

SIMPLE

Acupuncture is based on the fact that stimulation of the skin has powerful, health-inducing effects throughout the body. I have developed a stroking method which passes over many of the sensitive points along 'lines' or meridia (as shown by the arrows), so that a cumulative invigorating effect is produced. You will need a good moisturizing cream or oil to ensure that your fingers flow smoothly over your skin. Also make sure tht your nails do not scratch or cut the skin.

(1)

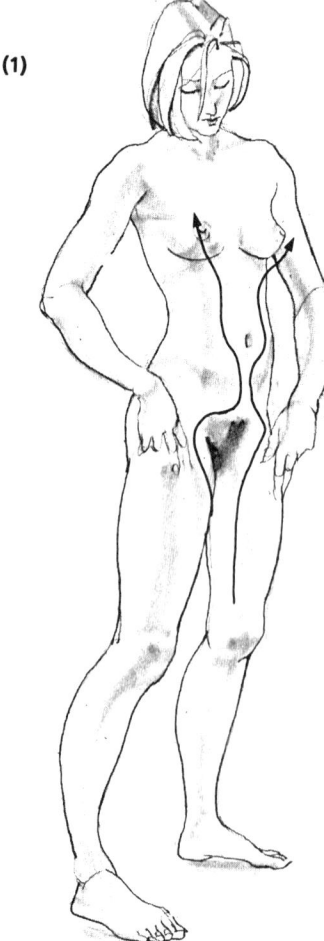

To start, stand with your feet apart and put your fingers on your knees bending at the waist. Press firmly and stroke along the lines shown, pressing on either side of your crotch, up over your pubic hair and diverging just before your navel (1). Continue up to your breasts and just stroke past your nipples on the edge nearest your arms. Repeat the whole sequence.

Having achieved a moderate degree of vaginal relaxation and lubrication, stand with your feet wide apart and your hands firmly on your buttocks. Then, following the line (as shown) up to your breasts, sweep your hands up your body and past your nipples, just touching your aureoles. Repeat, but this time thrust your pubic arch outwards.

ADVANCED

Once you have mastered the techniques described above for stroking meridia and have found the ones that suit you best, you can progress to an advanced use of these techniques which involves stimulation of certain key areas. These are effective in relieving sexual tension and also improve the skin tone. Some women report that they are helpful when dieting. They can also be used instead of vaginal or clitoral auto-release, or as a prelude to or interlude during auto-release exercises.

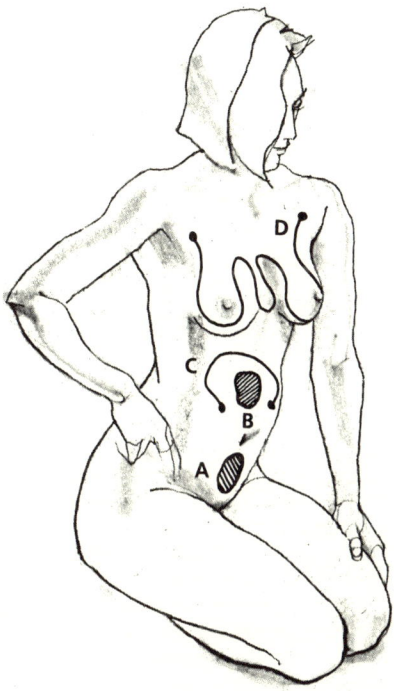

Areas A and B can be gently pressed with the fingertips. In some women the response is so immediate that it is as if 'a catch had been released' and tension flows away.

Follow the meridian C, then reverse. Make sure you are not rubbing against your rib cage – you can tell if you are because it feels hard. This movement should involve gentle pressure, but not against bone.

Stroke with your fingertips starting at D, and work across your chest to the parallel D area, then back to the starting point.

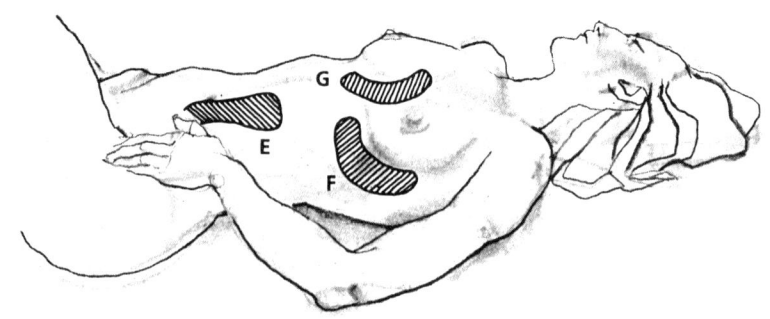

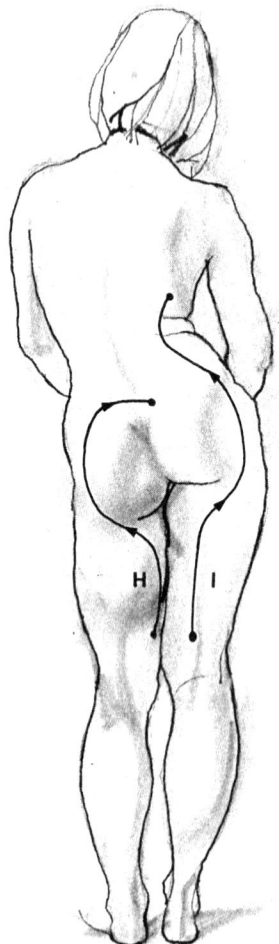

Start at the lower end of E, near the crotch, using the whole of the palm of your hand in upward strokes. This releases tension in the anus and increases the blood flow to the vagina and vulva.

Use your fingertips on F and G in backward and forward movements with very light pressure. Sensations up and down the spine usually result.

Use your fingertips for H, I, J, K and L, following direction of arrows only. Stronger effects are obtained by spreading the legs. Do this standing up.

Note that there is only one E, but two of F, G, H, I, K and L, one for each side of the body. Adept women double up, working on both Ks for instance at the same time. Even greater skill is needed, for example, to do an H when you are doing a K. Experiment and find what these powerful stimulators and relaxers can do for you.

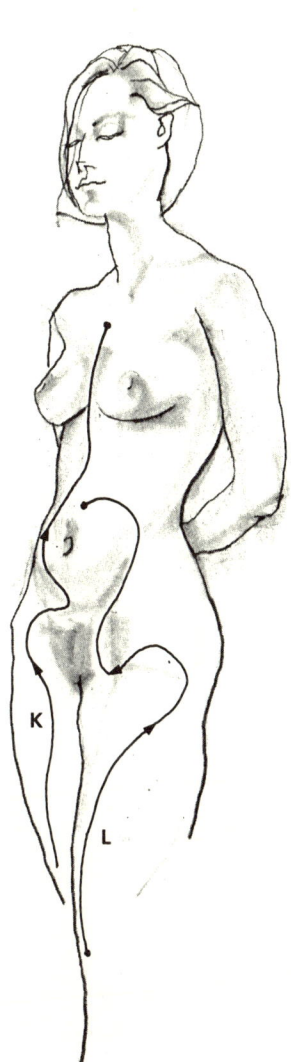

We found that one woman in two found these massage methods relaxing, while a small minority of women became tense – if you are in the latter group, do not use them until you have worked through the stronger methods – arching, heeling, squatting and deepeeing.

8. ROCKING

This is a difficult exercise to do well, so perform it carefully at first, very gently, and with no jerky movements. In addition, some women have such well-developed pubic arches that the movement can be uncomfortable without the protection of a cushion between the floor and pubic arch.

(1)

Lie face down, bend your legs at the knees and grasp your ankles firmly. Tense your whole body so that your back is bent like a bow (1). Keep your head up. Pull on your ankles which will enable you to perform a slight rocking movement on your tummy. Continue to rock backwards and forwards. As you do so, you will feel the muscles of your pelvic region tense and pleasurably relax. If you find that you cannot rock, open your legs wide, letting your buttocks relax, and 'hoot' your breath out. With practice you will be able to achieve greater curvature of the spine, but progress very gently.

9. BEACH EXERCISES

The purpose of these is to open your body to the air and sun. As excessive direct sunlight can be harmful to your skin, you should do the exercises, if possible, in shaded sun. They can be done on soft grass as well as sand, but if you find yourself on a nudist beach, so much the better.

(1)

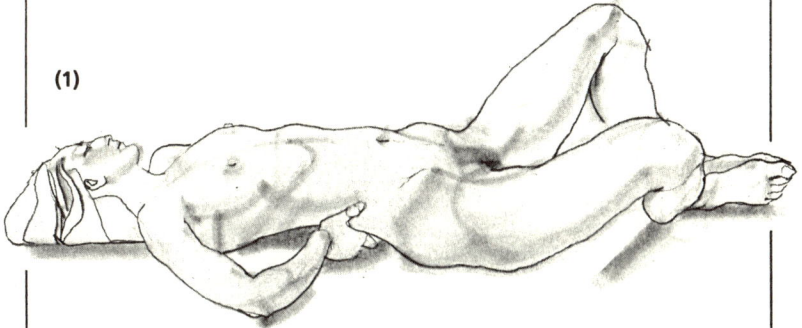

Lie on your back, draw your legs up and put the soles of your feet together so that your knees fall open, and place your hands underneath your waist. Breathe in and, as you do so, press your feet together and raise your waist off the ground by pushing up with your hands (1). Hold for a count of three and then relax. Continue the exercise until you feel a rush of pleasure to your tummy.

Still lying on your back lay your hands flat on the ground and raise your legs, bringing them up against your chest and breathing in as you do so (2). Hold for a count of three, then breathe out, stretching your legs flat out on to the ground. Continue until you are tense and then return to the preceding positions (1). You should find that the pleasure is now greater.

(2)

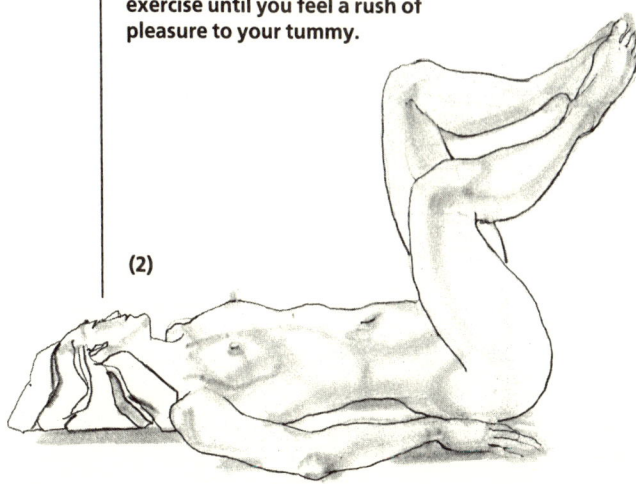

(3)

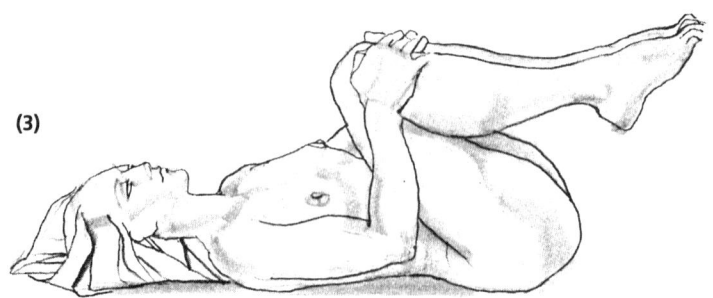

Lie on your back, lift your legs and pull your knees as close to your chest as possible, holding them with your hands and breathing in at the same time (3). Hold for a count of five. Stretch your hands and legs out on to the floor as you exhale. Repeat ten times. Continue until tense and then return to the position shown in illustration (1).

Stand as shown with your arms hanging loosely (4).

Then, raising your arms and moving the back leg forward, adopt the position illustrated (5). Lower your leg and arms and return to starting position (4). Repeat with other leg. This movement creates a small pressure down to the vagina and increases the blood flow to the breasts.

(4)   **(5)**

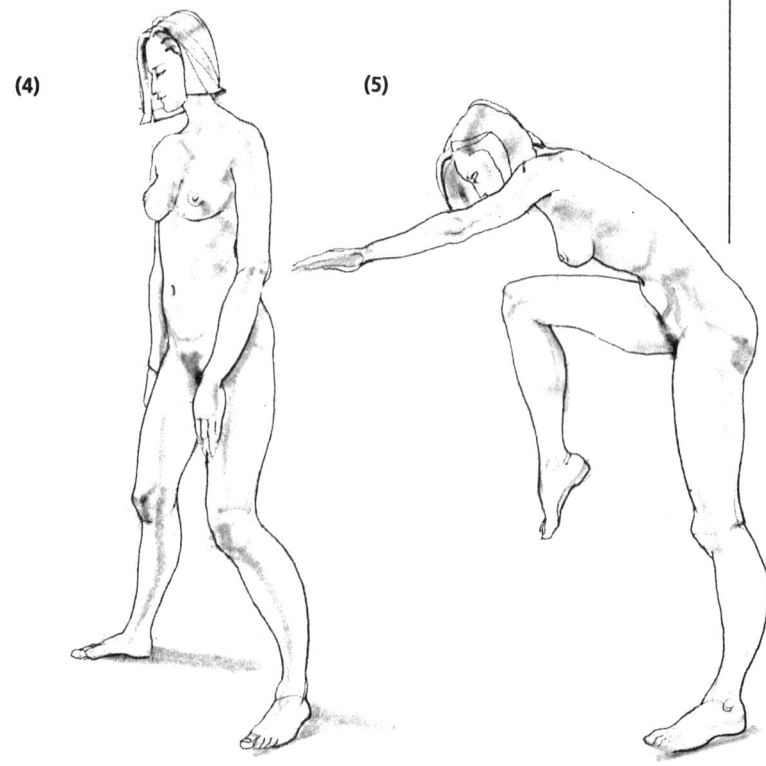

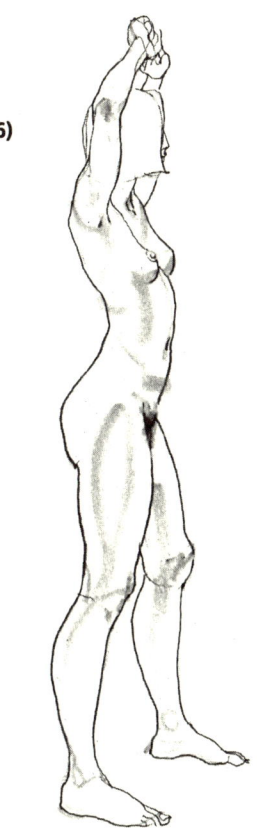

(6)

(7)

Stand with your legs apart and your arms folded in front of you. Raise your arms above your head (6) and then move your hips to the left and then to the right. This can be done to music. Relax your buttocks as you wiggle your hips.

Stand with your feet about 18ins apart. Take a deep breath and raise your left leg, grasping it firmly with both hands (7). Pull hard, then relax and repeat with the other leg. This is a good toner of the thigh muscles but also exerts a pull on the lower abdomen, thereby invigorating the vagina.

PART THREE: SPECIFIC EXERCISES

Your body must be regarded as a functioning whole, not as a collection of bits and pieces. However, by using movements which specifically energize certain areas or organs, the whole body benefits.

I have compiled exercises and methods in three broad areas: the head, which deals with the neck and face; the pectoral area, which energizes the breasts and chest and the pelvic area, which energizes and exercises the pelvic floor, the uterus and vaginal parts, the large intestine and the powerful muscles of the buttocks, thighs and abdomen.

SWIMMING is the ideal general exercise, but it also has possibilities in the Sexual Exercises area. The breast stroke is excellent for toning the muscles of the inner thigh and the opening of the vagina. The crawl strengthens the small of the back, and the back stroke invigorates the breasts. As your body weight decreases dramatically in water, all your energies can be concentrated on body movements.

Swimming in the nude permits a caressing flow of water over the whole body. As this sensual experience makes you more receptive to the deeper effects of powerful Sexual Exercises, it is better to swim *before* doing the exercises. Cold water may seem invigorating, but beware of cramp. Warm water is relaxing. You could try having a shower or a bath first.

MUSIC It has never been fully understood why music can give so much pleasure, not just intellectual or emotional but also sensual. That it does however, is certain. Tastes vary, of course. Some women enjoy Mozart operas, others prefer rock music. The key is to find which music relaxes you and to play it while exercising. Dreamy music appears to go better with massage, while a stronger beat is helpful in the more energetic exercises. Once you have learnt to associate certain music with your exercise routines, the music itself will induce the physical and mental state hitherto obtained through the exercises.

1. HEAD AND THROAT

Tension often strikes the throat first with a sensation of tightness and sometimes a hoarse or strangulated voice. The Sexual Exercises are specifically designed to alleviate tension, but if you find yourself somewhere where you cannot do the exercises, these facial movements will bring some relief, especially when done together in your own personal sequence.

SMILING

Smiling is so much part of our everyday life that a suggestion to practise it formally, as a method of alleviating tension may seen surprising. You will find, however, that a broad smile, repeated again and again, resolves mild tension very quickly. The rationale behind this is straightforward. We usually smile when we are happy and relaxed, and often when we feel sexually attracted to someone. Our reflexes are therefore conditioned to interpret good relaxed feelings with a smile, and this works in reverse. Smile and you will feel better.

COUGHING

When you cough, you exert pressure down on your vagina because the muscular wall of the diaphragm, which separates your chest cavity and your abdominal cavity, presses down. Coughing also stimulates the nerves along the rim of the rib cage. Obviously you should not force coughing but judiciously used this will relieve tension.

TONGUE WAGGLING

This exercise can be used to relieve tension in the lower part of your body. Poke your tongue right out and then rapidly push it back in and out. Then waggle it sideways from corner to corner of your mouth and you will feel a direct stimulation of your vagina.

TONGUE FLUTING

Flute your tongue and poke it between your lips with just the tip showing. Then suck. Keep this up until you can suck no more. Then open your mouth and waggle your tongue sideways. This has a direct effect on the vaginal nerves and the muscles of the pelvic floor, and is the basis for the myth that drinking alcohol in sips gets you drunker. It does not but the tiny sucks relax the pelvic floor and make the drinker feel mildly intoxicated.

Sometimes, if you are particularly tense, you may not feel any response in the lower part of your body with smiling, smacking, tongue waggling or fluting. In this case, you need to practise the more powerful exercises detailed in the section dealing with the pelvic area.

SMACKING

Pout your lips and make a smacking sound with them. Repeat this several times and use a wide smile. This is excellent for slowing down a build-up of tension in the throat and face but will not reach the tension blocks in the abdominal cavity.

SOUNDS

I discovered the relaxing and sexually enhancing effects of emitting sounds when I was investigating meditation. There are meaningless words called 'mantras' which meditators repeat over and over again, either audibly or to themselves. I became convinced that the mumbo-jumbo surrounding meditation ought not to influence one against its very real values. This was just as well because I found that making certain sounds vigorously has a profound effect on muscle tone and the flow of sexual pleasure.

Babies when happily at the breast hum and coo, as do men and women while making love. As the satisfaction increases, so do the sounds. The actual making of these noises heightens the pleasure.

UH!

Get down on all fours on a soft surface, spread your legs very wide apart at the knees and let your back sag so that your tummy relaxes. Now breathe in deeply and then exhale making an 'Uh' sound. Continue, until you can make an Uuuuuuuuu! which feels as if it starts from your tummy. You should find that your vagina opens and your buttocks relax. A wave of pleasure will start in the pit of your tummy, go to the base of your spine and travel up your back and to the front of your body.

AH!

Now try this sound. Do it a couple of dozen times in the same position as above. You will find that the effect is less powerful than Uh! but you may prefer it.

OOH!

The effect here is sharper and appears to start from the clitoris.

IH! AND EEH!

These appear to heighten sexual tension unlike Uh! which is more guttural and releases it.

Use these sounds alternately and vary them until you achieve the desired effect.

2. THE BREASTS

LIFTING

A supply of blood to the skin helps to maintain its sensitivity and suppleness, and the flow of blood to the breasts is crucial for health. This is a breast-lifting exercise and stimulates the circulation.

In a standing position with your feet 18ins apart, put your hands behind your neck. Press against your neck with your fingers, with your arms out.

Breathe out, then inhale and bring your elbows together in front of you. When you do this properly, you will notice that your breasts rise as you draw your arms together and fall as you spread your arms. Your nipples will enlarge, and the size of your breasts momentarily increase as the flow of blood increases. The effect on the muscles underneath your breasts persists long after the nipples have subsided and provides a strong muscular base for the breasts.

NIPPLING

Lie on your back with a cushion placed either in the small of your back or under your hips. Cross your arms and gently flick your nipples with your fingertips, using your left fingers on your right nipple and vice versa. Flick upwards and outwards, but not downwards. You may prefer to begin this exercise by doing one nipple at a time, but a more intense effect will be obtained by doing both together as described.

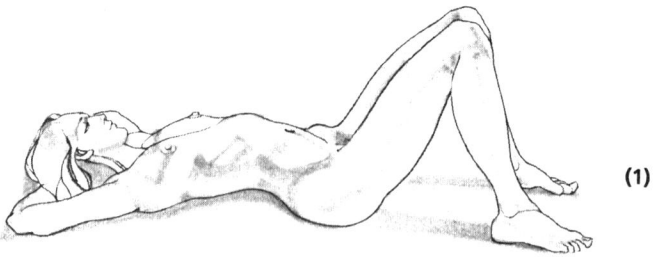

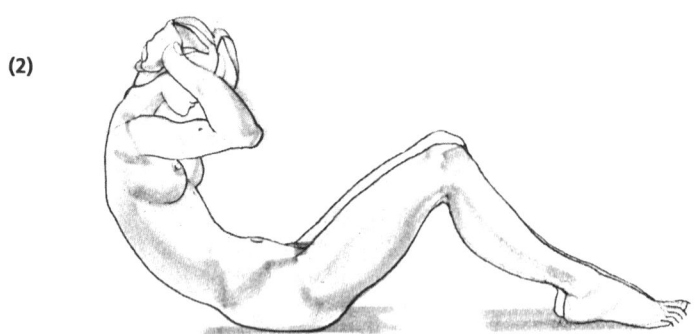

SNAPPING

This is a simple breast exercise. It also teaches co-ordination of the back and tummy muscles which are crucial for posture.

Lie on your back on a soft surface. Put your left hand under your head and massage your left breast with your right hand in a soft upward sweeping movement. Never massage downwards. Change over arms and repeat for the right breast. Muscles vary from woman to woman so watch yourself in the mirror to see how your breasts respond. Your nipples should stand out during the exercise, but if they do not, coax them out by tickling them lightly with your fingertips.

Still lying on your back but with your fingers interlaced at the back of your head, open your legs until they are between 18ins and 2ft apart. Then bend your knees and draw your heels up as close to your haunches as possible.

Raise your buttocks from the ground as far into the air as you possibly can, pushing your pubic arch upwards and out.

Without stopping the movement and when you have gone as far as you can, curl your buttocks down while arching your spine and thrusting your tummy upwards. To do this you must put a lot of weight on your back. In this way, when your buttocks touch the ground again, they will be some distance from your ankles, and your back will be raised away from the ground in an arch supported firmly at the shoulders (1).

Now, by tensing your tummy muscles and jerking your body towards your knees you will release the tension in your spine (2). When you lower your back to the ground, your spinal column will be flat and your head will have moved along several inches. Pull your heels back up to your haunches again and repeat.

(1)

(2)

(3)

BUSTING

This exercise increases circulation to the nipples and breasts. Good vaginal lubrication can also be obtained.

Kneel up and press your hands hard together (1).

As you breathe in, clench your knees together and sweep your arms above your head, falling back on your haunches as you do so. Then kneel up and exhale, relaxing your knees as you return your hands to the starting position.

Sit with your knees open and your hands placed on your thighs (2). Push hard on your knees until you are tired and then, as you exhale, let your legs relax and slip away from you until they lie flat on the ground. Do this ten times.

Sit with your hands round your knees (3). Try to pull your legs apart while, at the same time, tensing to keep them together. Let them open gradually, sighing hard as you do.

Now breathe in. Exhale as you pull your legs as wide apart as possible, and fall back on to a soft surface. This movement, repeated at least five times, stimulates the circulation in the breasts and frees the clitoris.

3. THE PELVIC AREA

PELVIC TONER Physical grace and balance imply mental poise. If you neglect your body, you are unlikely to achieve poise and serenity, but if you can learn movements which enhance physical grace, your mental equilibrium will benefit. Sexual health implies poise. This exercise, which is in three stages, is gentle, graceful and pleasurable to do. Learn each stage separately and then put them together at your own speed.

Controlling the line of your tummy is important in sexual health. To improve muscular tone, lie on your back and bring your knees up to your chest, pressing your knees hard against your hands. Increase the pressure until you begin to shake, then relax slowly. Begin this exercise very gently, otherwise you can strain a tendon.

(1)

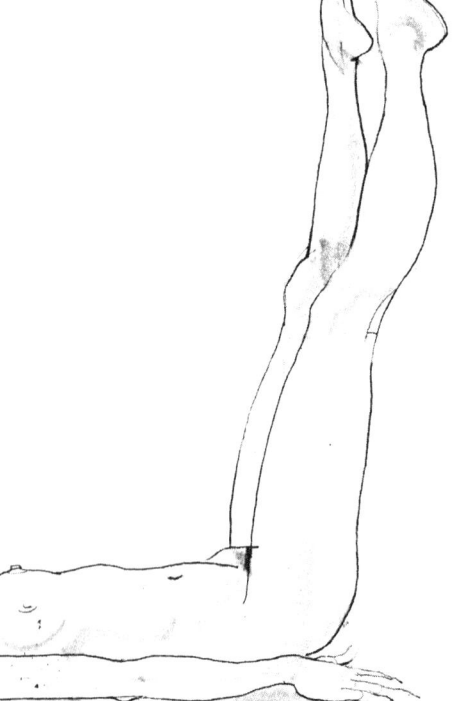

Once you get the idea, push your knees as far away from you as you can. Then pull your legs back against your hands as deeply against your chest as possible, as above. The aim is to balance your arm work against your upper thigh work as exactly as you can.

Once you master the rhythm, work for a minute or two. Then put your hands alongside your body, raise your legs in the air (1) and perform simultaneous circles with each leg. Push firmly with the palms of your hands on the floor to keep your legs straight up.

PELVIC PUSHING

Although women are very mobile in a lateral (side to side) movement of the hips, they are often weak in anterior/posterior (forwards and backwards) movements. The pelvic push will tone the muscles in your pelvis and tummy.

(1)

(2)

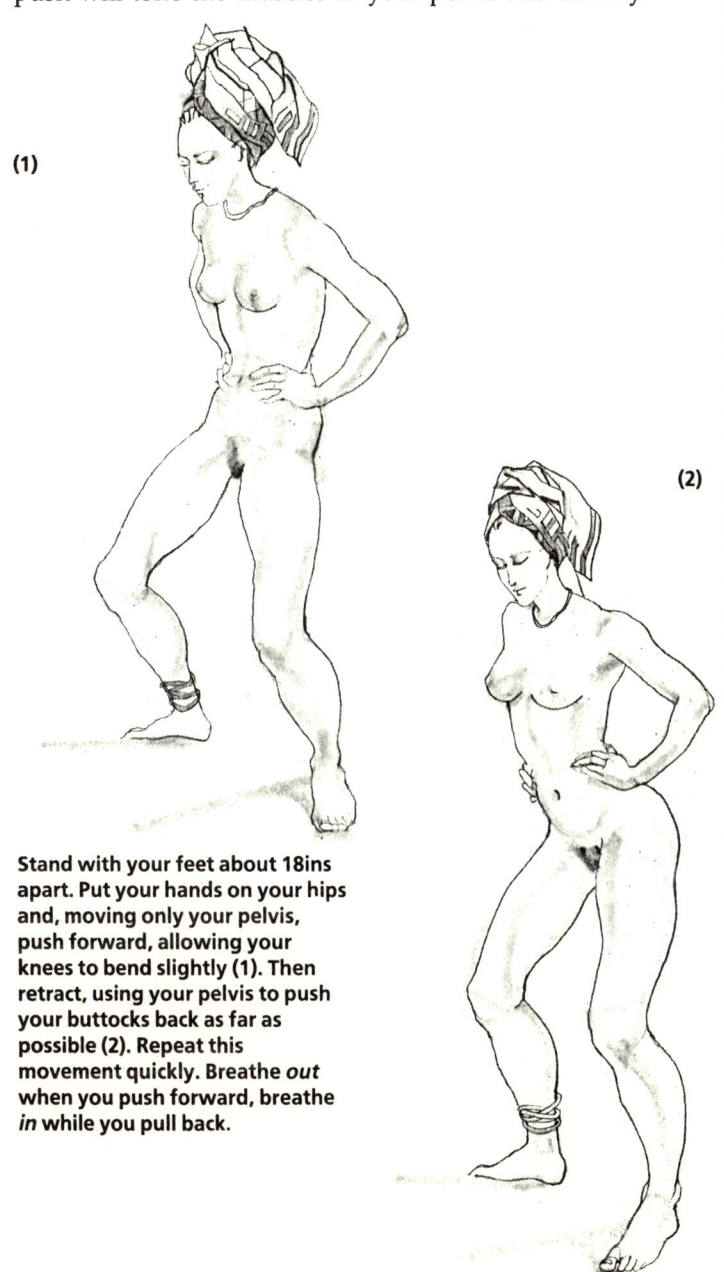

Stand with your feet about 18ins apart. Put your hands on your hips and, moving only your pelvis, push forward, allowing your knees to bend slightly (1). Then retract, using your pelvis to push your buttocks back as far as possible (2). Repeat this movement quickly. Breathe *out* when you push forward, breathe *in* while you pull back.

THE BELLY DANCE

I have modified this traditional Eastern dance into a useful sexual exercise because it is excellent for releasing tension in the pelvic floor, for toning the abdomen and for increasing the blood flow to the vagina. When done by experts, the buttocks also are controlled.

The health-giving power of belly dancing lies in its use of the pelvic girdle, the stomach muscles and the spreading of the legs. These induce intense relaxation and tension alternately in the abdomen, causing a warmth to radiate along the legs and back, from the sexual parts.

Advanced belly dancers have perfected the rippling of tummy muscles. I have not discussed this here as it is a complex art and usually requires considerable practice.

(1) **(2)**

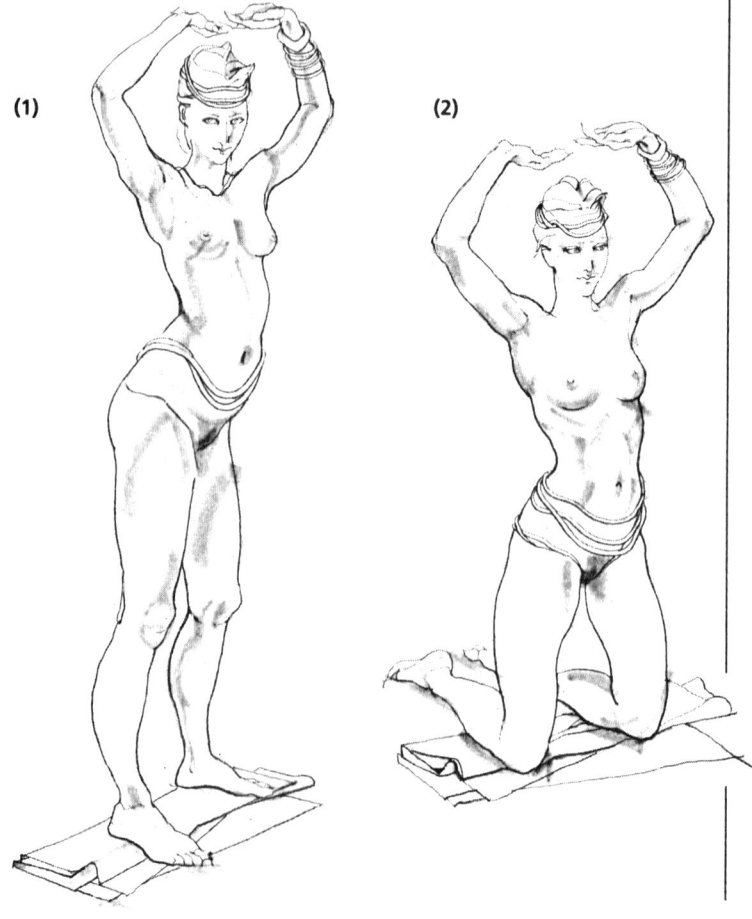

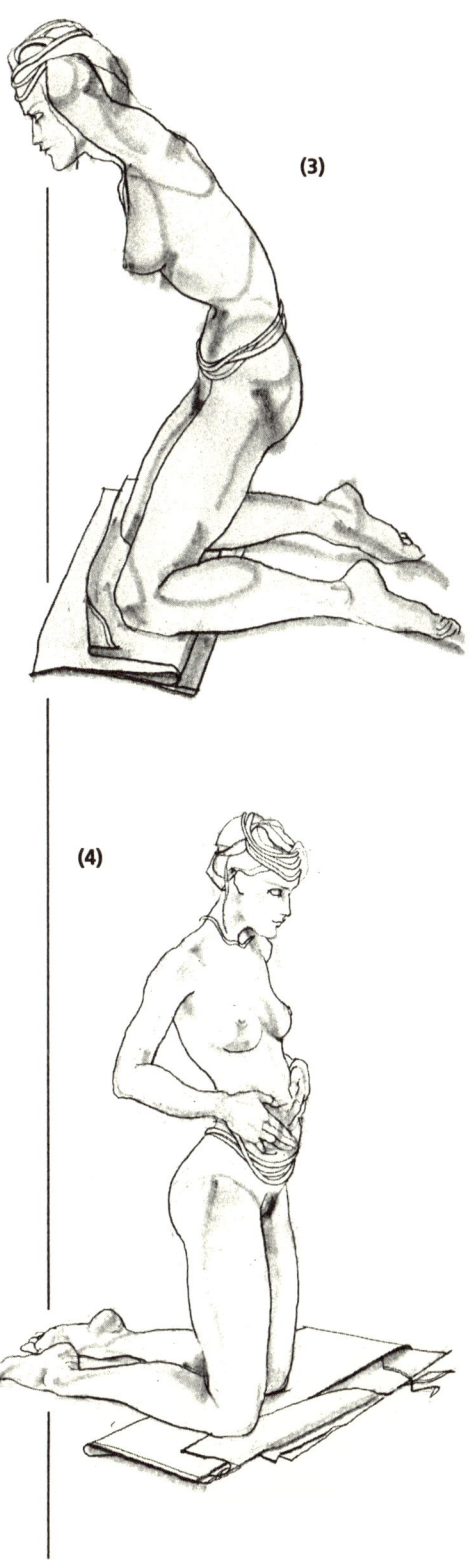

(3)

(4)

Stand with your legs slightly apart. Press your fingertips together above your head with the palms of your hands facing upwards (1). Breathe in and pretend you are pressing against the ceiling. Breathe out and relax. Keep the same position and continue to press towards the ceiling. Move your hips to the right, breathing in as you do. Return to the centre, breathing out. Repeat but moving to the left. Clench the muscles of your tummy rhythmically as you do this. In this position, push out the pubic arch firmly but slowly and pull your tummy in at the same time. Then pull the pubic arch back. Now do this while simultaneously rotating your hips.

Now kneel with your knees wide apart (2). Sink back on to your heels, breathing out and pressing the palms of your hands together above your head. As you kneel up again, breathe in and relax the palms of your hands.

Kneel with your hands clasped behind your neck and curve your body as far forward as possible while still remaining comfortable (3). Then do the same but leaning back. Pull your tummy in and out, and while clenching these muscles, gasp.

Kneel as before placing your hand on your tummy (4). Now breathe in deeply so that your tummy expands as you inhale. As you feel the expansion, massage your tummy with your fingertips. Sit on the floor with your knees wide apart and your feet tucked under your bottom. Clench the muscles of your tummy and hold the position for as long as is comfortable. Relax and then repeat the tummy massage.

THIGHING

This exercise causes the pubic arch to curve down and the spine to curve up. The buttocks and vulva also open during the exercise. In very healthy women, this process takes place within a few seconds of doing the exercise. In women who are more inhibited and less used to Sexual Exercises, it can take longer, but it is important to relax and respond to the exercise because it creates a high level of sexual ease, both when you are alone and with a partner.

Lie on your back with your knees bent and the soles of your feet against each other. Let your legs fall open by their own weight. Then stroke your thighs moving from your knee up towards your crotch and using both the fingers and palms of your hands (1). Breathe in as you stroke and breathe out when you move your hands back to your knees which should be done without touching your thighs. As you stroke, you will find your body responds as I have described.

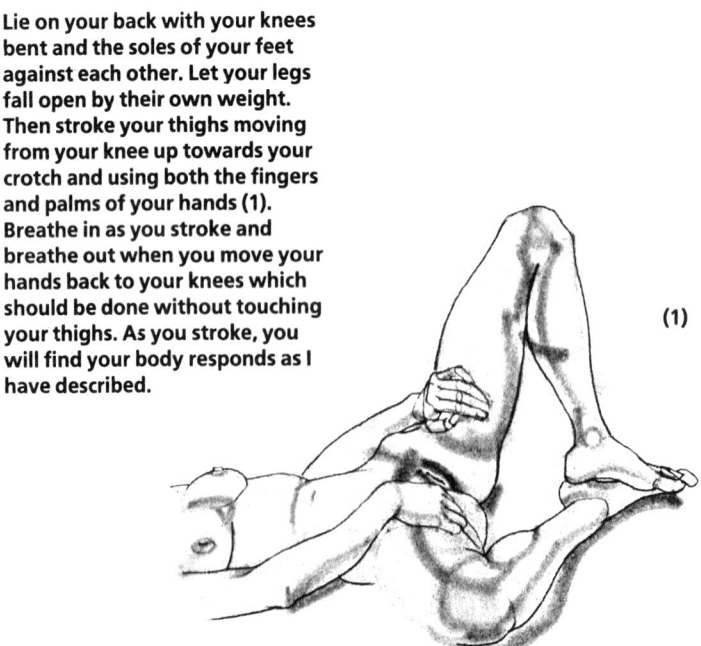

(1)

SPLAYING

This exercise beautifies the inner upper thigh which can often become slack through lack of exercise and, even if you are not overweight, sometimes collects fatty deposits. During the movement of the torso and legs, pressure is exerted downwards on the vagina, which causes pleasurable sensations, and the vagina itself opens and receives an air bath.

(1)

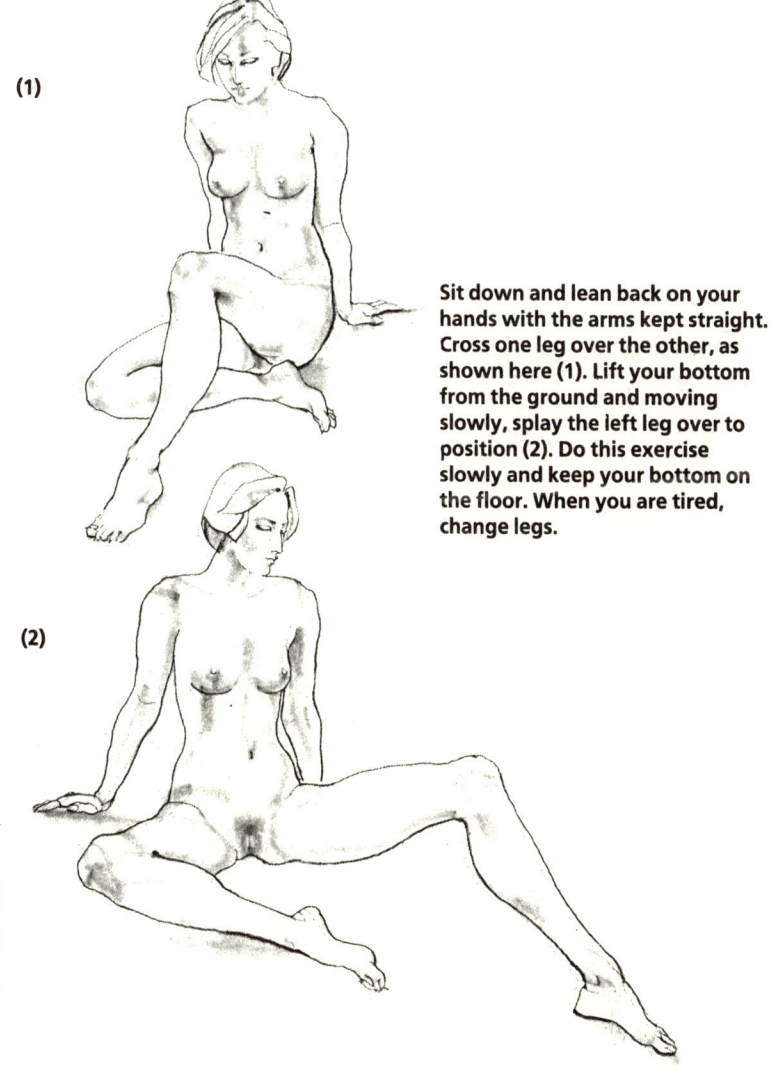

Sit down and lean back on your hands with the arms kept straight. Cross one leg over the other, as shown here (1). Lift your bottom from the ground and moving slowly, splay the left leg over to position (2). Do this exercise slowly and keep your bottom on the floor. When you are tired, change legs.

(2)

OPENING

This is a very basic and simple Sexual Exercise designed to increase your awareness of the inner structure of the pelvic region, in particular, the vaginal and uterine muscles.

Lie on your back, spread your legs, either keeping them straight or bending them, depending on which you find most comfortable, and gently prise the lips of the vagina open, by first pulling down on the thighs and by then moving your hands close to your crotch. Now draw your legs up till your feet touch your haunches. Then slide your feet back along the floor until you feel most comfortable.

Allow your legs to fall open without moving your feet again. Place your fingertips on your tummy, making sure that your shoulders are relaxed (1). You will feel a slight tension in the sinews of your inside leg. Now move around gently and you will soon discover a position that gives a pleasurable pull to your inner thighs. Once you have reached this state, you can concentrate on the front of your pelvic girdle, which is known as the pubic arch, or *mons veneris*. Thrust gently upwards while keeping your buttocks firmly on the ground.

N.B. Many women find this a rewarding position for intercourse and one in which orgasm is easily reached. This exercise, like splaying, allows the vagina to breathe.

(1)

VULVA RELAXATION AND OPENING

This exercise is a good test of your ability to relax and one woman in two finds it immediately pleasing. Use deepeeing with this exercise once you have achieved this position.

(1)

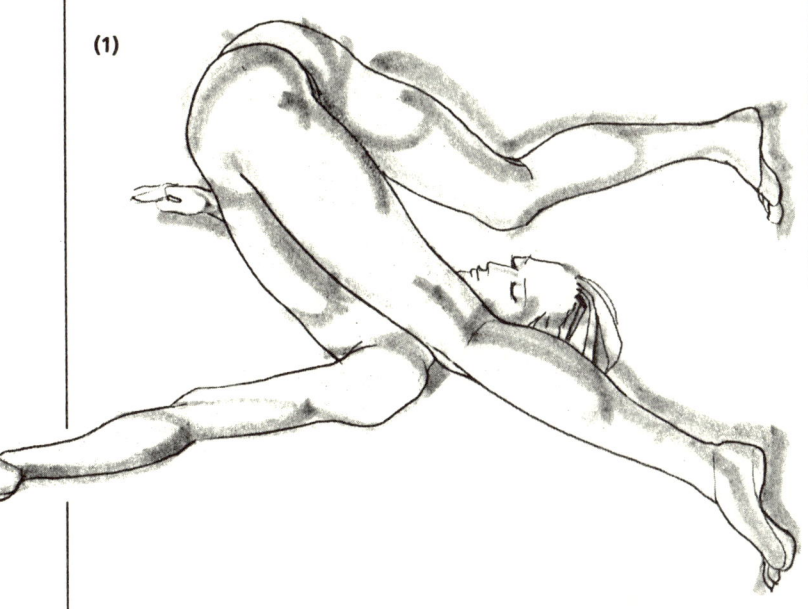

Lie down and bring your legs back over your shoulders as shown here. Your arms should be straight and your palms turned to the floor. Open your legs as wide as possible and gradually your knees will sink to the floor (1). This means that your body is relaxing. Check that your buttocks and the muscles of your vagina are not clenched. If they are, relax. As you get used to this position, you will find it very comfortable.

VULVA SQUEEZING

This exercise is a good firmer and toner of the buttocks and thighs.

(1)

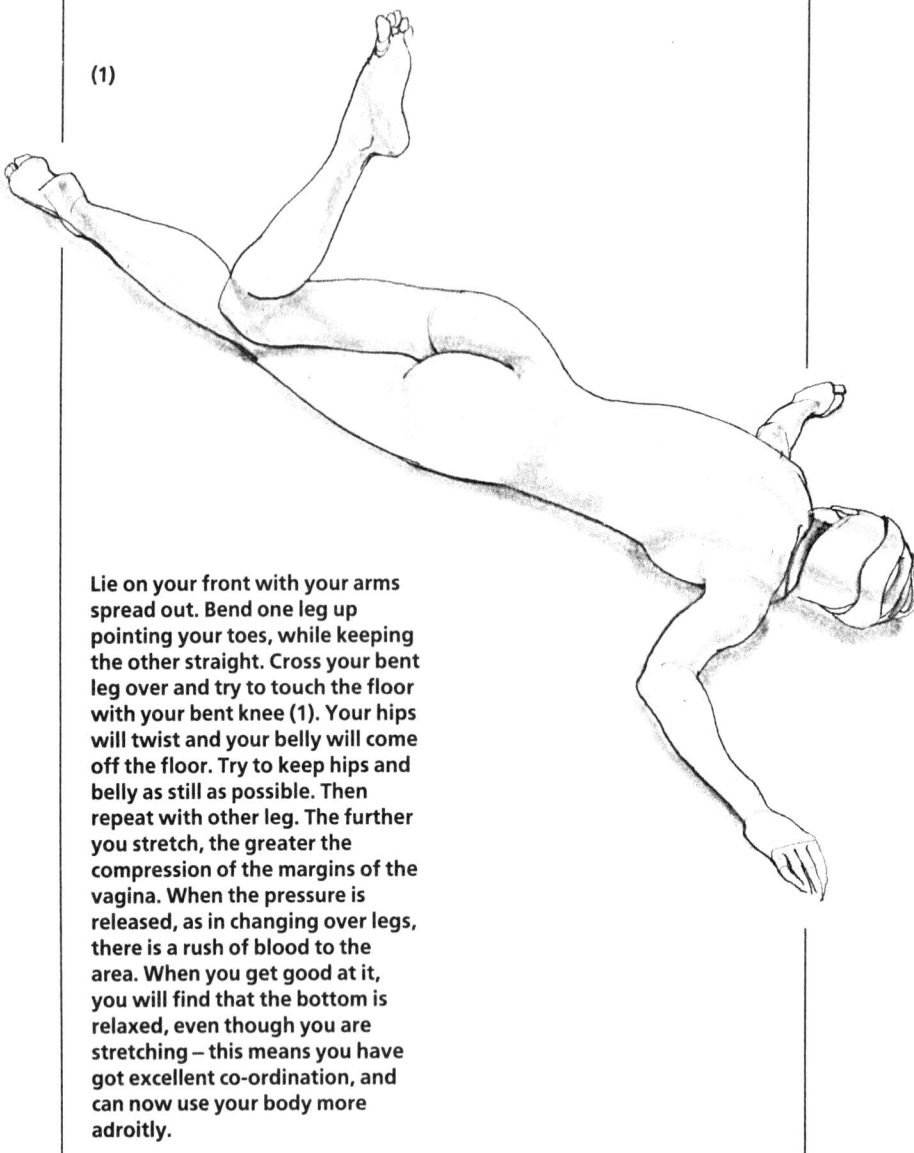

Lie on your front with your arms spread out. Bend one leg up pointing your toes, while keeping the other straight. Cross your bent leg over and try to touch the floor with your bent knee (1). Your hips will twist and your belly will come off the floor. Try to keep hips and belly as still as possible. Then repeat with other leg. The further you stretch, the greater the compression of the margins of the vagina. When the pressure is released, as in changing over legs, there is a rush of blood to the area. When you get good at it, you will find that the bottom is relaxed, even though you are stretching – this means you have got excellent co-ordination, and can now use your body more adroitly.

BOTTOM WORK

Among the most powerful muscles in the body are the gluteals, the muscles in the buttocks, and their wellbeing and fitness is essential to sexual health. By contracting them, you can achieve vaginal stimulation and control.

1. SPANKING This makes the buttocks tingle and the blood rush to the skin. A common side-effect is a sensation of warmth and relaxation in the vagina. Spank yourself. Do this in the shower to increase stimulation and blood circulation.

2. KNEADING The important nerve centres deep in the muscles of the buttocks are best stimulated by kneading. Again, it can be particularly enjoyable done under running water but, whether wet or dry, use some oil on the heel of your hand to help facilitate the exercise. Stroke down your buttocks and then grasp the flesh and pull it up. Initially, tension may cause you some discomfort, but as you unwind, this should pass. If it doesn't, do not continue the exerciser, but consult your doctor.

The next and stronger stage of the exercise involves gently opening the crevice of your buttocks. Breathe in as you do so and exhale as you let them come together again under their own elasticity. Then lie on your front, breathe in, press down, part your buttocks and gasp your breath out. The effect is strongly pleasurable.

ANAL RELAXATION

Healthy women can obtain pleasure, relaxation and ease from passing stools, provided their bowels are in good working order. Disorders such as constipation and diarrhoea are obviously uncomfortable. When touched, the healthy anus contracts. It is the sphincter, a ring of muscles, which does this. Tense people are already clenched unnaturally, and cramps result from such tension. After the initial spasm on touching, the healthy anus will relax. Gentle coaxing with a fingertip will cause it to relax and open still further. These exercises not only explore the erogenous potential of the anus, but also help to remove tension.

Cut your nails. Squat down. Insert a fingertip gently into your anus and push to the left. You will find that this may be pleasurable, but, at worst, you will experience a neutral sensation. You will feel pain only if you are tense or something is wrong. Pull towards the vagina. This is pleasurable, but if you pull away from the vagina, it often hurts. This is quite normal.

If you push your finger deeper into the anus and move it up and down, you will experience waves of pleasure across the pelvic floor. The anus will open even more and the sudden rush of blood to the vagina may be sufficiently powerful for you to feel jolted, so be gentle. Blood will also flow to your breasts and the lips of your mouth. Many women flush in their face, breasts and thighs.

N.B. We do not recommend the introduction of vibrators, dildoes or any other foreign objects into the anus, nor are we necessarily advising anal sex. That is a matter for personal choice. You should also be careful to wash your hands straight away after anal massage to ensure maximum hygiene.

DEEPEEING

Learning to control your urine flow is an important sexual exercise and has the additional benefit of exercising, among others, the pubococcygeal muscle, which forms part of the pelvic floor. The same muscles that can control the flow of urine are also responsible for opening, shutting and manipulating the entrance to and walls of your vagina.

It is best to do this exercise when your bladder is almost empty, as preventing yourself from urinating when you badly want to can cause tension. (Equally, women who are particularly sensitive in this region should be sure to relieve themselves before making love.) The loo is a good place to practise deepeeing, though the ideal situation is one in which you are able to squat down. Squat down or sit on the loo with your legs splayed. Urinate until your bladder is nearly empty, then clench your muscles to stem the flow. Relax, then repeat. Once you can do deepeeing, try it in *any* of the various Sexual Exercises throughout the book, with an empty bladder of course, to increase the effect of the exercise.

SQUATTING

Most women experience pleasure in the pit of their tummy after a few squats. Waves of relaxation will go up the inside of your legs and up from your crotch to your breasts.

(1)

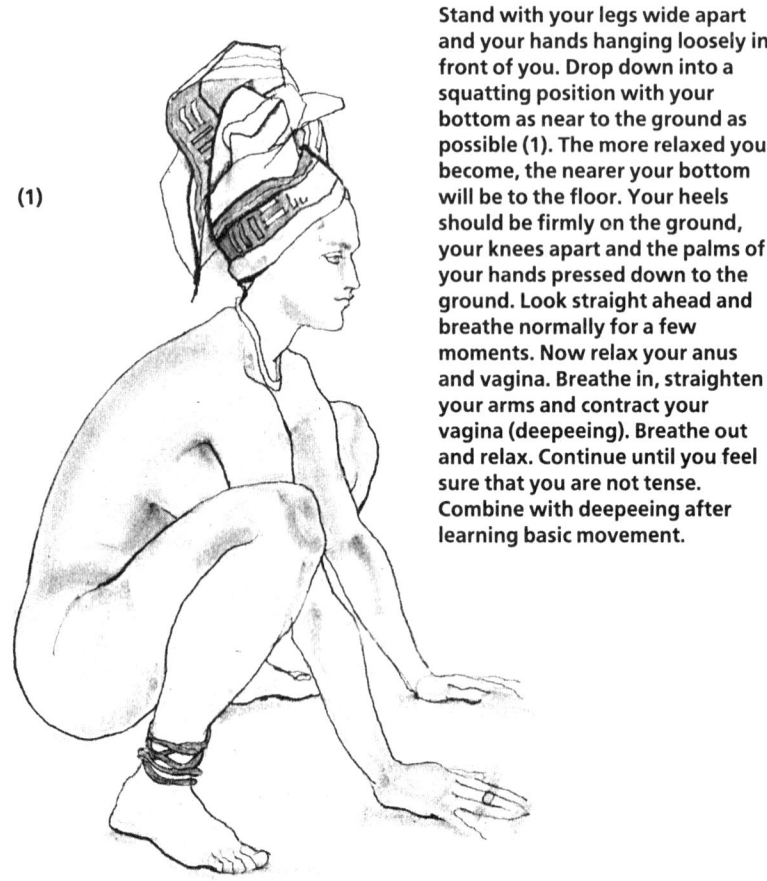

Stand with your legs wide apart and your hands hanging loosely in front of you. Drop down into a squatting position with your bottom as near to the ground as possible (1). The more relaxed you become, the nearer your bottom will be to the floor. Your heels should be firmly on the ground, your knees apart and the palms of your hands pressed down to the ground. Look straight ahead and breathe normally for a few moments. Now relax your anus and vagina. Breathe in, straighten your arms and contract your vagina (deepeeing). Breathe out and relax. Continue until you feel sure that you are not tense. Combine with deepeeing after learning basic movement.

PEELING

This exercise is good for the pelvic floor and vagina. To a lesser degree, it also benefits the breasts, increasing the blood flow and enlarging the nipples. It is similar to squatting but greater emphasis is given to curving the pubic arch up and forward.

Squat down with your hands flat on the floor. Press down inside as if you were going to the loo and push your pubic arch forward. Curl your 'tail' forward too.

Now relax, then tense the muscles of your vagina and breathe in as you stand up. As you rise, trace the line of your thighs, tummy and breasts with your fingertips until you are stretching as tall as you can. Breathe out as you slowly return to the squatting position, relaxing your vagina and buttocks, and pressing down inside as before. Now inhale and 'curl' again, as before.

QUIVERING

This is an exercise which leads to such a degree of relaxation that your tummy seems to cave in. Vaginal lubrication is moderate, but very warm, and the exercise is so deeply relaxing that many women fall asleep after doing it. It is therefore excellent just before going to bed.

Lie on your back with your knees raised as shown and wide apart and your arms relaxed and lying by your sides. Raise your bottom 3ins from the floor (1). Then put your bottom back on the floor again. Now start again, making sure that your feet are sufficiently far back so that you can touch your heels with your fingertips. Breathing gently and naturally, raise your hips by pressing upwards with your pubic arch. Move about half an inch upwards each time you take a breath. Change the position of your feet and legs until you feel most comfortable and begin to 'quiver'. Once you have found the right position, stay there. Keep breathing gently and put your arms behind your head. When you get tired, rest your hips on the floor.

(1)

HEELING

This means the use of the heel of your hand to massage the vaginal tract from the outside. Once you have done the quivering' exercise, while still in the 'quiver' position (see p. 81), place the heel of your hand on your tummy just below the navel and press gently. Massage by sliding it down to your pubic arch slowly. You may find a moisturizing cream or lotion helpful.

GEEING

This exercise involves stimulation of the G-Spot and can often lead to orgasm. The G-Spot (or Grafenberg area, called after the doctor who first identified it) is still the subject of controversy and discussion, but what is beyond dispute is that stimulation of the area just inside the vagina and above the pubic bone, leads to sexual arousal and can cause orgasm.

Prior stimulation of the vagina can be done by heeling (see above). However, before geeing, it is advisable to urinate as a common response to this kind of intense stimulation is a desire to urinate. Either adopt a squatting position or sit in a low chair with your legs splayed. Insert two fingers into your vagina, pushing up against your pubic bone and away from your backbone. Press down with your muscles against your hand. A little exploration will soon tell you which area responds to the stimulation. If you use your other hand to stimulate your clitoris and vaginal lips, you reach orgasm very quickly. Some women find that their pelvic floor relaxes during stimulation, while others report feeling their uterus contract, and relax.

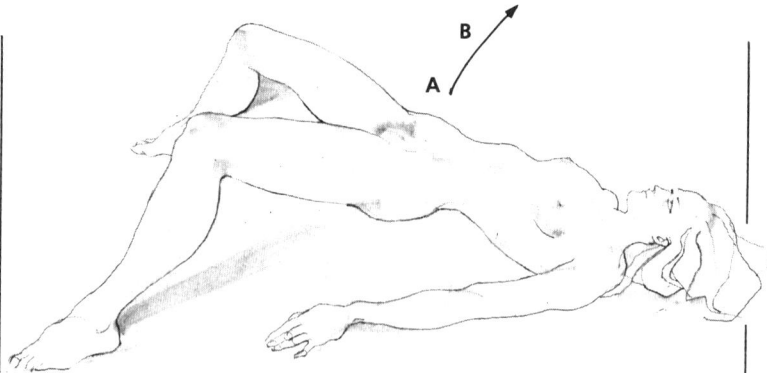

HALF-ARCH

This is a powerful vaginal lubricator which is also very relaxing. It can be used in conjunction with nippling.

Lie on your back with your hands at your sides, palms facing down, and with your legs bent at the knees, and with your feet about two feet apart.

Breathe in and press on your hands and feet to raise your hips from the floor. Breathe in gently as you lift yourself steadily up, taking at least five seconds. When you reach the top of the arch (A), push upwards as high as you can, at which point you feel the weight transfer to your shoulders and your hands will relax, and hold your breath for a count of five. Then exhale by hooting, taking at least ten seconds to exhale completely as you descend, returning to the first position.

Give in to the pleasurable sensations this produces, and repeat at least twelve times, developing your own rhythm to bring you maximum pleasure. Then repeat, but add vaginal and anal clenching as you rise into the arch position and relax as you come down.

ARCHING

This exercise uses a position similar to that in quivering, but it requires greater control because of the movement involved and when done well you will find that you go up on your toes.

Lie on your back with your knees bent and wide apart. Breathe in steadily on a count of five as you push upward with your pubic arch (B). Hold this position while you count three. Then exhale and come down slowly to the first position. Repeat several times.

Now repeat, but tense your vaginal muscles, clench your buttocks as you push your pubic arch up and pull your tummy in, making it hollow at the top of the arch. This time, rise on to the balls of your feet, bringing the feet nearer your buttocks, and consciously splay your knees. As you come down, relax your buttocks and vaginal muscles. Try to open your vaginal lips. Increase the pace until you are going up and down very quickly. Remember to breathe in as you go up and out as you come down.

COOLING

After a busy day wearing clothes in confined spaces, the body is often overheated and sexually excited. The cooling exercises exploit the fact that when the vaginal and anal areas are suffused with blood, they swell and expand. Cooling effects can therefore be obtained which are very relaxing. The exercise also floods your body with pleasure-inducing hormones, creating even greater relaxation.

(1)

Lie naked on your tummy on a soft but firm surface with your arms and legs comfortably on the ground, but with your knees bent and apart (1).

Point your toes and breathe in. Now pull your toes towards your back, bending your knees as much as possible. Make an effort to relax your back. You will find that your hips naturally lift off the ground. Continue to breathe in and press your feet strongly towards your back (2).

Hold for a count of three and then breathe out, letting your feet sink slowly back to the floor and relaxing your toes. Let your pubic arch come to rest back on the floor and spread your legs as wide open as possible. Repeat.

(2)

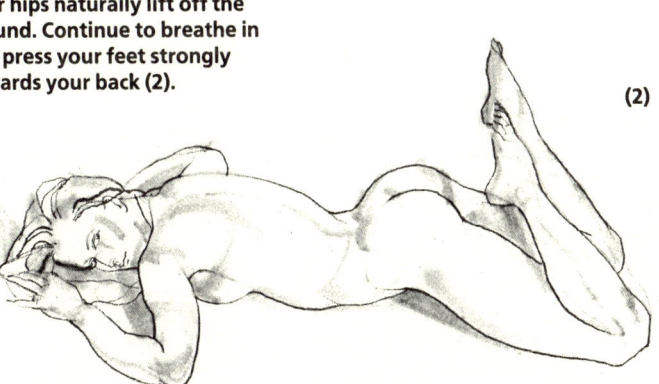

ALL FOURS

This is a very powerful exercise and many women reach orgasm quickly by doing it. The most common response is considerable vaginal lubrication and a pleasurable feeling in the tummy and vagina. Try it out gently at first and, if you experience any discomfort, desist.

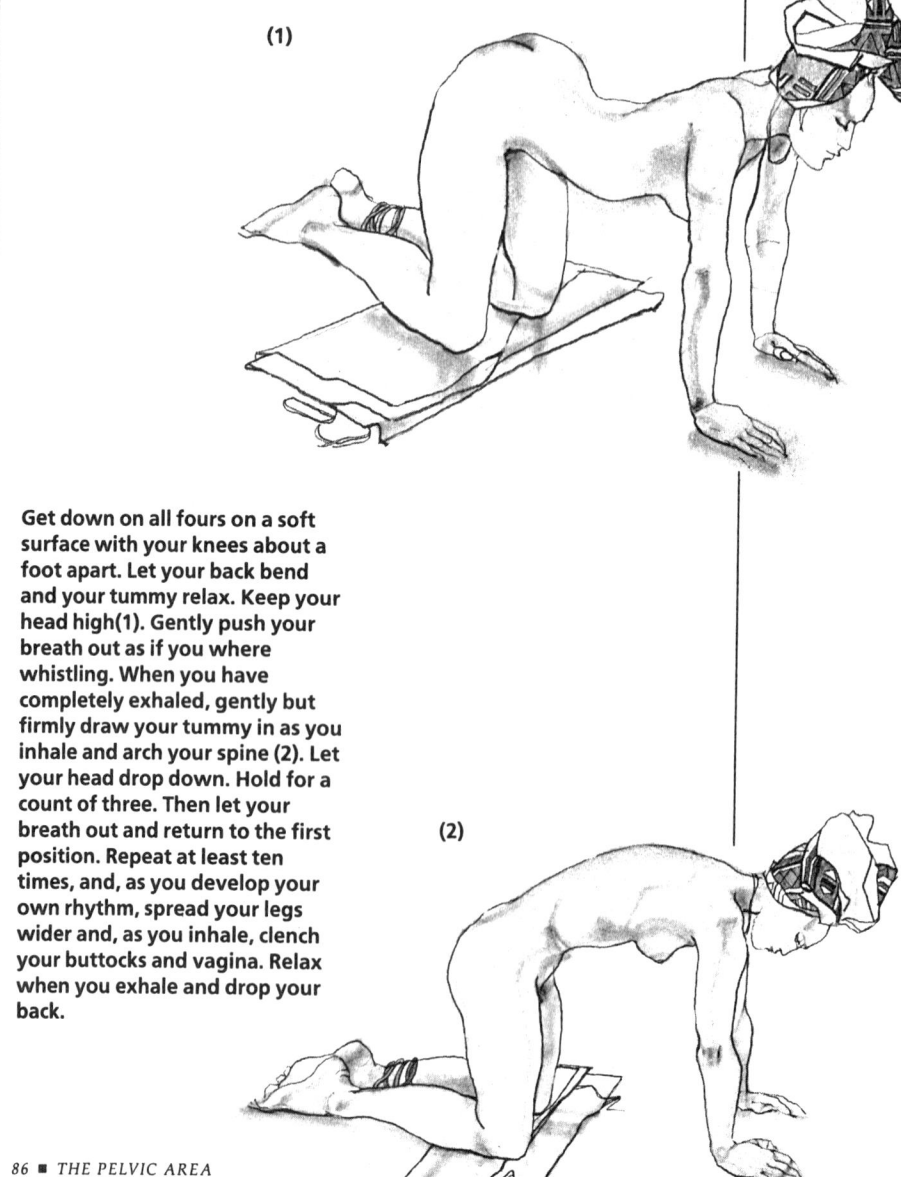

(1)

(2)

Get down on all fours on a soft surface with your knees about a foot apart. Let your back bend and your tummy relax. Keep your head high(1). Gently push your breath out as if you where whistling. When you have completely exhaled, gently but firmly draw your tummy in as you inhale and arch your spine (2). Let your head drop down. Hold for a count of three. Then let your breath out and return to the first position. Repeat at least ten times, and, as you develop your own rhythm, spread your legs wider and, as you inhale, clench your buttocks and vagina. Relax when you exhale and drop your back.

AUTO-RELEASE

The point of Sexual Exercises is improved health, relaxation and pleasurable body sensations. For some women, auto-release is not only a natural and intrinsic part of this, but also the physiological conclusion to the exercises.

You will soon evolve your own methods of auto-release and discover what gives you most pleasure, but these simple exercises should put you on the right track.

Lie on your back, on a bed or a soft rug or even in the garden if it is warm enough. Let your legs part. Stroke your vaginal lips gently with your fingertips. If you have warmed up with some Sexual Exercises, you should already be lubricated and ready. If, however, you are a little dry, you can moisten yourself either with your own saliva or a surgical jelly. Tease your clitoris with your fingertips once it has swollen in response to your stimulation.

TO INCREASE YOUR RESPONSE 1. Put your feet together, sole against sole, and push hard, synchronizing the stroking of your vagina with the push. Arch your body upwards and breathe deeply.

2. While one hand caresses the vulva, the other should press against the area between the navel and the pubic arch. This induces deeper orgasmic release.

3. Put a cushion under your bottom to arch the spine. This is a more comfortable and open position.

4. While you stimulate yourself, stroke the lips of your mouth with your fingertips or tongue. Massage your nipples and squeeze your breasts.

APPENDICES

1. BODY TYPES AND THEIR NEEDS

The shape of your body is one of a number of factors that have considerable bearing on sexual health and pleasure. But not every woman knows how to unleash her potential for pleasure. Many women, for instance, have thin upper bodies and heavy lower ones, and feel uncomfortable about the disparity between the two. This is unnecessary, as health unifies your body. Use Sexual Exercises – particularly the more powerful routines like arching or squatting – to learn how to release the pleasure in your body. In time, you will learn which exercises suit you best. A flow of blood to the breasts is vital for their health, and women who have large breasts should take special care and pay particular attention to the breast exercises described in Part Three. Women with powerful upper bodies may well find that their main area of sexual response is pectoral, rather than pelvic.

SLENDER WOMEN Thin women are more prone to the muscular tension which Sexual Exercises can reduce. Women of this type usually respond quickly to their own stroking and massage because the sensory areas are closer together on a smaller body and the skin is thinner. When a thin woman is healthy, her flow of sexual energy is extremely rapid and she will get to know her body very easily and quickly. Slender body types have ankles which are about 8½" round the thinnest point, and wrists of 6" or less. Their features are often aquiline, their arms and legs long, their shoulders high, their hips narrow, and all their bones are long and slender. Their skin is thin, too. At 5'6", this body type weighs up to 8st.

MUSCULAR WOMEN Muscular women tend to suffer less from muscular tension. This is probably because their muscles are so strong that they can sustain more nervous stress. However, when tension does occur, it takes much longer to relieve than in a woman of small or even average build. More heavily-built women find the more powerful exercises (such as arching and squatting) most effective, as they need to work hard to get the circulation going deep in the tissues. The muscular body types have ankles often more than 9" round and wrists more than 7". Their hips and shoulders are wide, the waist is often high and not clearly defined because they become overweight. Their bones and joints are strong and their features are strongly moulded. This body type is often very athletic and many power athletes are in this category, while women runners are usually slender. The muscular women often weight 10st at 5'6".

NATURALLY PLUMP WOMEN Described as Renoiresque, these women often have pert and pretty features, luxurious hair, small hands and feet, wide hips and generous bosoms but tiny waists. The rounded body type has narrow, high shoulders. Ankles and wrists are often slender. Usually these women dislike strenuous sports but are often excellent swimmers. They respond well to self-massage and stroking, and to the deeper exercises, and they are very supple in their spines and joints. If you belong to this group, you will receive maximum pleasure from Sexual Exercises, but the effects are often slow to come. The secret is not to be in a hurry.
Sexual Exercises lead to a higher average rate of energy expenditure. Physical effort can vary from sedentary, which uses up two calories per minute, to heavy labour, using eight or more calories per minute. The immediate slimming effect in itself is minimal, but, because exercise puts the body into a higher rate of energy use for many hours afterwards, exercises do help you to slim. Put simply, exercise can put you into a higher metabolic gear. However, tense underweight women *put on weight*, because the release of calming hormones, which have been previously inhibited, appears to reduce their average energy expenditure.
Usually, small-boned slender women maintain a good balance between eating and energy output. They tend

to eat less when less active and eat more when more active. These are the people who seem to be able to eat what they like and get away with it. The danger is that often they do not eat well enough.

The rounded person who gets more and more overweight seems to suffer from an inbuilt imbalance, so she eats even when she does not need to, perhaps because she enjoys it so much.

Women of average build have a good energy balance, but can easily slip into a pattern of slightly overeating so that they very gradually put on weight.

2. WEIGHT

How much should you weigh to be sexually healthy and fit? The weight of your bones will remain constant once you have stopped growing, which, on average, is at about the age of fifteen. Provided you are in good health, your internal organs will weigh only as much as is necessary for them to function effectively, and the only deviation from this is likely to be during menstruation and pregnancy when different physiological needs operate. The weight of your muscles should be whatever is sufficient to enable you to work and play effectively.

But once the layer of fat beneath your skin is thick enough to make the skin sag because the weight is too great for its elasticity, then you are overweight. Conversely, if the layer of fat is too thin, then you will be underweight.

To gauge whether you are the correct weight for sexual health, you have to take into account not only how much you weigh, but also the quality of your skin and the thickness of the fat underneath. A woman of large skeletal frame who is 5'5" with a 40–28–42 figure and weighs 10st, but has no wrinkles in her skin, no sagging and no more than ½" slack when she pinches herself, is not overweight. She is perfect for her body size. But a woman who at 5'5", weighs 8½st with wrinkles, sagging tummy and thighs and with ¾" flesh pinch on her arms, can be overweight, particularly if she has small bones and rib cage. The measurements for this kind of figure will read 34–29–35, with the weight in the belly and arms.

BREAST SIZE A woman worries as much about the size of her breasts as a man traditionally worries about the size of his penis, but, in both cases, there is not much to be done, and a better relationship with your body is the best way to reduce the worry.

White, black and brown women tend to have larger breasts than Oriental women, but these differences are minimized when they have been brought up on the same diet. The most common breast size is a B cup; 50% of women have this, while 25% are A; 15% C, and 10% D. It is unlikely that both your breasts will be the same size, and the right breast is usually larger in right-handed women, a fact that bra-makers do not appear to have registered.

The shape and size of your breasts is affected by fluid and hormone levels, particularly during menstruation and pregnancy. Sexually active women tend to have firmer, healthier breasts, and this can also be affected by diet. Breast fat is harder and less svelte when you eat a lot of animal fat but is softer and smoother if you eat vegetable oils. You can improve the condition of your breasts by massaging oils into the skin.

AVERAGE SIZES About one in two American and European women take a size 14–16 and measure 2" more on the hips than the breasts.

THE TABLES About two women in three can use the measurements as shown, but tall women (5'7"+) and short women (less than 5'3") will need to adjust bust, waist, hips and thighs by about ½" for each inch difference in height, adding for tall women, subtracting for short women. The other measurements vary less: ½" for the arms and pelvic width, ¼" for the wrist and ankles, per inch in height.

Weights vary about 4lbs per inch of height for slim, medium, and athletic builds, 5lbs per inch for the naturally plump or rounded. If, for example, you are 5'9" and of medium build, you add 3" of height to 5'6", giving three lots of 4lbs, which is 12lbs, giving your weight as 142lbs.

Healthy deviation from these weights occurs when:

1. Your breasts are large; add 2lbs for C cup, 4 for D cup, and 5 for E cup bras.
2. You have exceptionally well-developed *firm* thighs. Add 3lbs below 5'5", 5lbs to 5'7", and 6lbs thereafter.
3. You have exceptionally well-developed shoulders and arms; add as for thighs.

In both cases 2 and 3, well-developed means firm smooth contours, with no sag.

HOW AND WHAT TO MEASURE Bone measurements assess your skeletal frame:

HEIGHT: Stand bare-footed against a wall, put a book on your head, making sure it is level, and mark the wall with a pencil where the underedge of the book meets the wall. Measure with a tape from the floor to the pencil mark.

WRIST: You should measure at the thinnest part, on the nearside of your wrist bone (nearest to your body), with your hand open.

ANKLE: At the thinnest part when you are standing, just above the ankle bone.

The other measurements reveal how much muscle and soft tissue you have: these change when you get overweight or too thin.

Note that you half-inhale for bust measurements, *relax* your tummy for the waist measurement.

Now put your measurements in Table 2.

Now compare, after adjusting for your height, your measurements with the values in the table of guide measurements. Write in S, M, A, C where your measurement fits most closely (if in the middle take the next one up). If you fit most of the measurements of one you have a good structure to work with already.

TABLE 1
WOMEN OF 25 YEARS: BODY MEASUREMENTS IN INCHES

BODY AND FRAME	S SLIM	M MEDIUM	A ATHLETIC	C CURVY
Bust	34	36	38	40
Waist	23	24	26	28
Hips	35	37	38	41
⎰ Wrist	6	6¼	6½	6¾
⎱ Ankle	8¼	8½	8¾	9
Upper thigh	20½	22	23	24
Weight (pounds)	115	130	135	146
Stones	8st 3lbs	9st 4lbs	9st 9lbs	10st 6lbs

The two bracketed measurements are frame measurements, which are fixed in adulthood. These, along with height, determine what frame size or body type you are. The other measurements vary according to life habits. The above values are for a height of 5'6" and are indicative of sound structure and weight. (Adapted from the author's *Human Measurement*, Heinemann Educational Books, 1978.)

TABLE 2
YOUR MEASUREMENTS Write in here slim **S**, medium **M**, athletic **A**, curvy **C** from comparing your measurements to those in Table 1. Most women have mixed figures and we have found that this leads to different sexual needs and habits.

Bust

Waist

Hips

Wrist

Ankle

Upper thigh

Weight

Height

3. DIET

It is far better to be slightly overweight but strong and robust than to be too thin from a diet which lacks adequate vitamins. Even so, the advantages of a well-covered, but not overweight, and well-functioning body are well worth the time and effort necessary to acquire it. Sexual Exercises have often stopped women from going on food binges by channelling the energies and enthusiasms that might have been directed towards food into physical exercise.

Eating well means four small meals a day. In a day you should eat: dairy produce, fish or meat, fruit, nuts, vegetables and cereals. Try to eat fresh food rather than frozen, tinned or processed, and, above all, vary your diet.

Women who menstruate heavily (about one woman in ten does) should endeavour to eat steak and/or liver once a week. Spinach is also a good source of iron as is a glass of red wine. Green salads increase your body's ability to absorb iron from meat and fish.

HIGH STANDARD NUTRITION We found that progress in Sexual Exercises was always faster when the diet was adequate. You need grilled lean meat; white fish; two or three boiled eggs a week; 4oz of liver; skimmed milk and some cheese for high-quality protein which is good for your skin and a general sense of physical wellbeing. Eggs and liver supply the B vitamins (beneficial to nerves, hair and skin). Dairy produce provides vitamins A and D which help your bones and skin. You need fruit and vegetables for vitamin C and for fibre content. Fibre tones the internal muscles of the body and cuts down fat absorption. Finally, you need wholegrain cereals, such as brown rice or wheat germ, for minerals, plant oils and vitamin B. White bread, sugar and fatty foods are not so beneficial.

To benefit most from good foods, eat often, four meals a day – most fat people nibble all day and end up with a binge before going to bed. A good breakfast consisting of cereal, skimmed milk, a boiled egg or grilled bacon, and fresh fruit, is essential for maintaining the nutritive intake and calorie balance.

It is impossible to get fat on fresh fruit. You would need to eat 20lbs of it a day just to build up enough to get through the twenty-four hours. So when you are hungry, fruit should be the food to which you turn. Boiled vegetables are also non-fattening.

CALORIE CONTROL This means eating as many calories as you need. If you eat more calories than you use in your work and play, you put on weight, while if you eat fewer, you lose weight because you burn up existing fat. Good calorie control is necessary in order to get the best out of Sexual Exercises because obesity appears to diminish sensuality. However, some women are naturally plump. If you are one of these the area to watch is the tummy. Ten inches difference between waist and hips is a good target.

VITAMINS Because these are needed in such small quantities, their importance is often underestimated. But, just as the tiny jewel bearings in a watch are essential, yet contribute very little to its total weight, so vitamins are crucial to the human body.

The other problem with vitamins is that there are so many of them, but we still tend to rely on pure chance to get enough of them by eating a varied diet. Human sexuality is based on adequate levels of daily vitamin intake because if this is disturbed, you lose these jewels of sensuality through your urine. This is particularly true of the nerve- and mood-balancing vitamins, vitamin C and the vitamin B complex.

A good diet, which will provide about 250 milligrams of vitamin C, consists of a daily consumption of a fresh salad, two to three apples, two oranges and some freshly cooked vegetables. This degree of vitamin C intake fully saturates the blood and tissues. If, however, you are taking the Pill, you should consume more of these foods because the Pill appears to destroy this vitamin.

Research has shown that insufficient levels of vitamin B lead to irritability and lack of drive and libido, and if the deficiency is allowed to continue, more serious diseases can develop. Vitamin B levels can be boosted by the following: liver once a week; brown rice; wholemeal bread; brewer's yeast; wholegrain rice; wholegrain cereals.

VITAMIN	WHERE TO GET IT	WHAT IT DOES
vitamin C	fresh oranges, all fruits and vegetables	protects against colds, 'flu, keeps skin young, especially lips, eyes, nipples, sexual organs
vitamin E	wholewheat bread, wheat germ oil	improves hair, guards against the effects of city air on your skin, in your lungs, increases volume of semen in men, and stimulates vaginal juices
vitamin B Group niacin	brewer's yeast, bread, liver	for energy, for skin, guards against depression and irritability
B12	food of animal origin	protects against anaemia
folic acid	green vegetable leaves	helps prevent anaemia, keeps tissues healthy, perhaps the most widely deficient vitamin in women
pantothenic acid	eggs, liver, milk	burns fat for energy
thiamine	lean pork, wheat germ, oil	for energy and nervous functions

VITAMIN	WHERE TO GET IT	WHAT IT DOES
riboflavin	cheese, eggs	skin health, helps resistance to common facial infections
pyridoxine	whole grains, leafy green vegetables	helps hair health and vitality
carotenes (which makes vitamin A)	tomatoes, peaches, carrots	healthy bones
ergosterol dehydrocholesterol	yeast, edible fungi, liver, animal fat	these materials with sunlight form Vitamin D
D vitamins	animal and fish livers, and oils from them	essential for healthy bones

FATS The condition of your skin and the contours of your body depend on fat. Plant oils, nuts, the skins of fruits and vegetables, liver and fish contain very varied types of beneficial fat. Cream, butter, milk and yoghurt also contribute to the wide range of fats essential to our health and wellbeing. The animal fats contained in fatty meat, suet, lard and dripping are not particularly beneficial when eaten to excess.

Vitamins A, D, E and K are fatty in their nature. Even cholesterol is necessary to manufacture the sex hormones, but in far smaller quantities than we actually consume. An excessive intake of fat of any kind is unhealthy. Your diet should contain the widest variety of nutritional sources for maximum sexual health.

Oils useful in cooking are sunflower seed oil; olive oil; safflower seed oil; wheat germ oil; corn oil (from corn on the cob) and peanut oil.

Fats are slightly acidic in nature but do not dissolve easily in water. The fat content of your skin prevents it from becoming excessively dry, and the actual quality of your facial and body skin depends on lecithins, which are used to make smooth surface skin cells. Lecithins are a component of all body cells, and are found in concentrated form in egg yolks, liver and brains.

Like most of your body, nerves are three-quarters water. Fat is the next most important constituent of the brain. You depend on nerve fibres to send and receive messages to and from the brain to various parts of the body. Each fibre is encased in a fatty sheath which protects it and plays a part in conducting the nervous impulses which are translated by the brain into pleasure, scent, touch and other senses.

MINERALS The great difference between minerals and other foods is that there is no substitute for them. Whereas sugars can be obtained from proteins and fats from sugars, iron cannot be made from magnesium nor sodium from potassium.

Most of the essential minerals are widely dispersed in our foods. We should therefore have little difficulty in obtaining adequate amounts of each but complications are caused by our dietary reliance on sucrose, white flour and excessive amounts of salt. Here is a guide to minerals, their sources and their benefits.

Mg MAGNESIUM: Our bodies contain between 20 and 25 grams of magnesium, most of it in bone. Sources are cereals, meat and fresh vegetables. Alcoholic drinks in excess can increase magnesium loss from the body and severe magnesium loss can result in muscle tremor, delirium and even convulsions.

K POTASSIUM: Potassium is linked to fluid balance. There are adequate supplies in meats and vegetables, but most other foods tend to be high in sodium as well and this can lead to an imbalance of sodium to potassium. Levels of potassium are very much affected by stress. Shock leaks potassium into the blood from the cells and potassium deficiency causes muscle weakness, poor heart function and irritability.

Na SODIUM and Cl CHLORIDE: Salt – sodium chloride – is essential for health but an excess unbalances other minerals. Once the precise balance in the tissues of important minerals is disturbed, muscular strength, co-ordination and the function of the nervous system are upset.

Most tinned and convenience foods tend to be high in sodium.

Ca CALCIUM: Although our bodies contain between 1 and 1½ kilogrammes of calcium, most of it is in the bones. It is, however, also essential for the working of the nervous system and the clotting of the blood. You may be getting one-fifth of your daily calcium requirement from hard water. You depend mainly on dairy produce for the rest.

Se SELENIUM: The effect of vitamin E is enhanced by selenium, and both are essential for growth, tissue health and fertility. It is not fully understood how it works but, because of its relationship with vitamin E, it is thought to keep down the level of peroxide in the tissues. Peroxide is a poison which is formed naturally and can cause tissue damage. Wheatgerm is an important natural source of vitamin E and is not found in white flour or bread. Much of the selenium in vegetables is lost in the cooking water.

I IODINE: It is not certain how much iodine we need every day but about 200 microgrammes seems safe. It is especially important for pregnant and lactating women, and children. Iodized salt is easily obtainable from supermarkets. Most dairy products contain small amounts of iodine. Seafood is a good source. When iodine is not obtained in sufficient quantities, various goitres can result. Iodine is an essential constituent of the hormones from the thyroid gland in the neck which regulates heat production and energy levels in the body. The thyroid function is particularly important for stability of mood; women tend to be more vulnerable to goitres than men.

Co COBALT: This metal is at the heart of vitamin B12. It is found in liver and other animal foods. Cobalt deficiency causes lassitude and serious forms of anaemia.

Cu COPPER: You need about 2 milligrammes of copper a day. The distribution of copper is rather similar in foods to that of iron and if a diet is low in iron, it tends also to be low in copper. Blood disfunction with attendant lassitude is caused not only by B12 deficiency but also by inadequate supplies of copper.

Mn MANGANESE: Manganese is essential for sexual development and important in building enzymes which help to oxidize sugars and provide energy. Manganese salts are usually coloured; there is a higher concentration of manganese in the coloured parts of the eye than in the rest. It is found in nuts, cereals, legumes and leafy vegetables which contain about twenty parts of manganese per million parts. Dried fruits, fresh fruits, non-leafy vegetables, meat and poultry products contain between one and five parts manganese per million, but fish and dairy products contain very much less. Wholewheat flour contains about thirty-one parts per million while white flour contains only five parts per million. If half the calories you consume are supplied by white flour, manganese intake may be restricted.

Fe IRON: Red blood corpuscles contain haemoglobin, at the heart of which is iron. Without iron, haemoglobin cannot function as an oxygen carrier. In the other body cells, iron has a variety of different functions but a partial lack of it causes tiredness and a greater deficiency results in breathlessness and palpitations. A nutrient is useless until it enters the bloodstream and one way to get a good absorption of iron is to eat meat with salads and all fruits with a high vitamin C content. An intake of orange juice will help you to absorb iron. Ability to absorb iron varies from person to person.

F FLUORINE: Fluoride is included in minute amounts in the structure of the teeth as it is a component of the crystalline matrix of the outer parts. In a good diet and with water supplies containing the natural fluoride salts obtained from rocks and soils, adequate amounts are usually acquired. Lack of fluoride in itself does not cause tooth and bone decay, but if there is a fluoride deficiency, sugar causes decay more easily. Fluoridation of water supplies is achieved by the addition of fluoride salts.

S SULPHUR: If your protein intake is adequate, then so will your intake of sulphur be as it is part of the essential components of proteins. It also functions in the respiratory process. Sources are meat, fish, eggs, beans and cereals.

P PHOSPHORUS: This is essential to the structure of the bones and teeth, the storage of energy in the muscles and as a key constituent of the genes. It is found in proteins, meat, fish and dairy produce. Deficiencies are rare except in diet lacking variety, but many confections and refined foods contain very little.

Zn ZINC: Zinc is required in such small quantities that its importance was only recently realized. It is an irreplaceable constituent of the mechanisms which maintain the level of respiratory waste products in our bloodstreams at bearable levels. The zinc levels in our blood fluctuate and fall rapidly under conditions of stress. Phytic acid, which is found in wholewheat bread, interferes with zinc absorption, so a diet of hamburgers and cereals, for example, which contain phytic acid, would certainly supply too little zinc. If roast beef scores 100 for zinc content, then white bread scores ten, wholewheat bread twenty (the phytic acid reduces some, but not all of the availability of the zinc), potatoes ten, and fruit and vegetables generally between one and five. Burns and wounds heal more quickly with the consumption of zinc salts, particularly if the diet has previously been low in zinc. The effects of zinc deficiency are insomnia; anxiety; diminution of skin elasticity leading to stretch marks; loss of hair; loss of sense of smell and taste; failure to menstruate during adolescence.

Cr CHROMIUM: This is needed to maintain adequate levels of glucose in the blood and to protect against diabetes. We receive most of our chromium from our mothers, and as a result, women who have had two or more children usually have less chromium in their tissues than other women. Chromium is increasingly difficult to obtain in adequate quantities in Western diets because, like many trace elements, it is concentrated in the outer layers of cereals and is lost in the milling process necessary to produce white flour. Chromium is also lost in sugar refining, as is shown by the fact that there are significant amounts in brown sugar and molasses, but effectively none in white sugar.

4. LIST OF EXERCISES

FINE WORKS OF NON-FICTION AVAILABLE IN QUALITY PAPERBACK EDITIONS FROM CARROLL & GRAF